Rain Maker Pro

Rain Maker Pro

A Manager's Guide for Training Salespeople

Clifton Warren

BEP

BUSINESS EXPERT PRESS

Leader in applied, concise business books

Rain Maker Pro: A Manager's Guide for Training Salespeople

Cover design by Charlene Kronstedt

Interior design by Exeter Premedia Services Private Ltd., Chennai, India

First published in 2021 by
Business Expert Press, LLC
222 East 46th Street, New York, NY 10017
www.businessexpertpress.com

ISBN-13: 978-1-63742-046-1 (paperback)
ISBN-13: 978-1-63742-047-8 (e-book)

Business Expert Press Selling and Sales Force Management Collection

Collection ISSN: 2161-8909 (print)
Collection ISSN: 2161-8917 (electronic)

First edition: 2021

10 9 8 7 6 5 4 3 2 1

In memory of
Jordan Thomas Warren
(1996–2019)
You are always in my heart

Description

Generating leads and landing new business are critical to the growth and long-term success of any type of service business. Rain makers who are able to consistently gain new business by using their selling skills to convert prospects into new customers are difficult to find. Recruiting rainmaking professionals from other organizations is expensive and for many businesses has been largely ineffective.

Every executive and manager of a service business understands the importance of the ability to generate leads and landing new customers are the critical components to a successful business. This book is written for managers and leaders who want to transform their professionals from doing work to effectively marketing and selling and bringing in new business.

Divided into three comprehensive parts: Charting a new course; The fundamental success models; and Building your business, this book will show you how to:

- Help professionals overcome fear of selling
- Acquire the right sales capabilities
- Market and sell within your comfort zone
- Setting and achieving big goals
- Leverage existing customers to acquire new ones
- Build accountability across the business

Keywords

rain making; account development; lead generation; marketing; attracting new customers; selling; sales pipeline; sales tactics; referral marketing; sales training; accountability

Contents

Acknowledgments

Completing this book has been a challenge and has taken much longer than I ever expected. During the writing of this book, I had to deal with family tragedies, adjust business to global pandemic conditions, whilst rain making and adding value to my clients. I would like to thank all of my clients, friends, subscribers, and supporters of my work for providing a constant learning lab that has helped me to continually improve my knowledge and expertise enabling me to add value and help so many others.

Thank you to my publisher Business Expert Press for the opportunity and support to publish my third book. To Nicole, Kallen, Somraudee, and Sze Ting, you keep me smiling and laughing. Finally, thank you to Cheryl for her patience, support, and providing the freedom from distraction to allow me to write this book.

Introduction

Selling is the oldest profession in the world and a critical fundamental for a successful business. Every service business needs people who are able to generate leads, convert those leads into new customers who will remaining loyal advocates for many years.

Once upon a time, to generate new business could hire a salesperson, provide a telephone and the yellow pages to generate appointments. When we needed to purchase a product or service, the salesperson was the source of all the knowledge. For example, when you contacted an insurance company to purchase coverage for your house and car, you were directed to your local neighborhood broker who was the source of all the knowledge. When you wanted to travel, you contacted a local travel agency to discuss your plans. Today, insurance companies and airlines compete directly with insurance brokers and travel agents, respectively.

Competition across many service industry sectors is rapidly changing the increasing commoditization of many products and services is a challenge for business to business (B2B) services. Buyers today are smarter and able to access information from their computers, tablets, and phones without having to speak with a traditional salesperson.

In the last 15 years, there have been wars, as global financial crisis, and a worldwide pandemic that has contributed to this change. So how do accounting, finance, insurance, engineer, law, and other professionals attract, develop, and retain profitable business?

Enter the rain maker, a term professional services have been using since the 1970s. The term avoids the word selling, which some professionals often find distasteful. Rain makers generate revenue and profits and create opportunities for service business to growth organically, whilst producing opportunities for others to do important work. Rain makers are in big demand and most organizations are unclear how to get them. They constantly search for the elusive person who will generate new business for everyone. Some hire technical people hoping that a few will turn into rain makers. Some try to lure hired guns away from competitors—this is seldom effective, as they know little about the organizations past success, until they learn. A person who was a successful rain maker at one place is seldom able to repeat their success somewhere else.

Rain makers are different from traditional salespeople. Rain makers develop strong networks and powerful relationships, they match a prospect's needs, opportunities, frustrations, and challenges with their organization's capabilities to attract prospects. They are customer centric and results focused. Many people believe that salespeople are born and not made. I believe that almost any professional can learn to become an effective rain maker, however, many organizations simply don't know how to do it.

This book is written for people who manage and lead professionals, and who want to develop their professionals into effective business developers and rain makers. It will help the managers to create the necessary environment what needs to be done to develop those skills.

This book will also provide guidance to those professionals who want and need to learn how to become to be rain makers, such as independent professionals. It compliments my first book, Financial Services Sales Handbook, which was written for the individual professional who wanted to make the transition from doing work to selling it.

This book has three parts. Part I defines what is a rain maker, dispels myths and false beliefs, and covers the rain maker mindset. Part II covers four success frame works required for successful selling and rain making. Part III covers developing and executing action plans, achieving big goals, and success. The appendices cover additional techniques, guidelines, and checklist to implement this program for your organization.

PART I

Why You Need to Chart a New Course

CHAPTER 1

What Exactly Is a Rain Maker?

We are all salesmen everyday of our lives. We are selling our ideas, our plans, our enthusiasms to those with whom we come in contact
—Charles M. Schwab

Think of rain makmaking as a metaphor for money, it is the highest form of new business development that can provide a business with a distinct competitive advantage in a crowded marketplace.

If you want to train, coach, and develop your professionals into rain makers, it helps to know and understand what a rain maker is and what they do. A rain maker is a person who generates revenue and profits by bringing new business.

The term rain maker dates back to the Native American Indians, who practiced dancing to encourage rain for the necessary crops, particularly in summertime when there was a drought. The rain maker would dance and sing songs in the plains, the activity was believed by others in the tribe to cause clouds to come and be brought to life to give rain. Similarly, a business rain maker is a person who brings in new businesses. Just like the native American Indians' rain dance, rain makers' work can appear to work like magic.

Service firms often use the term rain making to distinguish from the word selling, which some may find distasteful. Every business requires new customers for the long-term growth and survival.

In smaller organizations, this responsibility often falls on the owner. In a medium to large organization, there will be several individuals and teams who will often have this responsibility either as a full-time business developer or part of their job responsibilities will include generating a certain amount of new business each year. For aspiring professionals working in service firms, an essential item on their to-do lists is business development to progress their career.

Bright technical people are always available; however, talented rain makers are in short supply. I have found many businesses that are great with the technical stuff and lousy at developing their marketing and sales capabilities to produce new customers.

Their focus is often on attracting young talent, assigning existing client responsibilities, and hope with some luck that some will develop into effective new business developers. Others try to hire specialist sales guns (rain makers) from competitors or other industries, and this is often expensive and dangerous as these hired guns often know little about the culture, past work of the business or product knowledge. Professionals who were successful in another company are often unable to replicate their prior success for their new employer.

Another challenge, rain makers' work can be seen as a mystery, especially if you are not in sales, you don't quite understand how they work, generate activity, and bring in new business—it just sort of happens.

The purpose of this book is to demystify rain making and provide an approach for executives and leaders to develop their professionals from doing work into effective rain makers.

What Are the Different Types of Sales Professionals?

Business-to-business selling (B2B), sales professionals can be classified into three categories as shown in Figure 1.1.

Farmers

Farmers take care of existing customers that have been assigned to them; their job is to provide first class customer service to ensure they are satisfied, and their business is retained. Some farmers may have revenue targets to achieve (growth from existing clients) and good farmers are capable of identifying existing customers' needs, providing and presenting solutions to close new revenue opportunities with these customers. Farmers who are less skilled will often pass these opportunities to someone else (a hunter) to close.

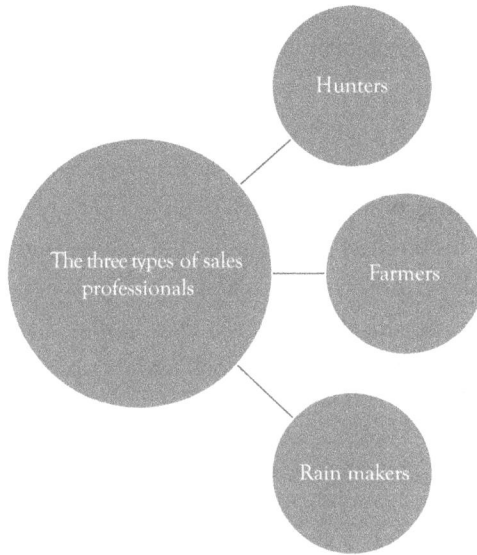

Figure 1.1 Categories of sales professionals

Betty works as a client relationship manager for an independent insurance agency. She has 14 years of experience and is responsible for clients who generate less than $1,000 in annual revenue. She has 350 clients in her portfolio generating over $300,000 yearly revenues. She knows all of her clients personally and is fully qualified to advise clients on their additional needs. When one of her long-term business clients mentioned they were planning several overseas business trips, she spotted an opportunity, Betty quickly provides a quotation and arranges the cover—generating an additional $1100 in new revenue for the agency.

Hunters

Hunters are skilled at connecting opportunities and closing businesses. Hunters are prospectors looking for new business, and occasionally this happens internally (farmers providing a lead). Usually, it is through reaching out to prospective clients via e-mail, phone, cold calling, and networking. Hunters work the law of averages X number of appointments equals Y number of sales. They may have a portfolio of existing customers to look after, however, their primary responsibility is new business generation.

Bill is a business development manager for a business process outsourcing (BPO) firm. His ideal clients are businesses who could benefit from outsourcing their back office customer service functions (call center) to improve profitability. Bill knows that for every 20 contacts, he will obtain five meetings of which one will result in a sale over time. He generates most of his business opportunities through networking and cold calling. Bill only focuses on new business; after he successfully acquires a new client, he passes this along to a client relationship manager (farmer) for ongoing service. This frees Bill to look for new opportunities.

Rain makers

Rain makers focus on relationship building, combining the skills of a hunter and farmer to build a web of connections and establish strong personal and business relationships. Rain makers are able to spot opportunities at the conceptual stage and convert them into customers and new revenue. Rain makers focus on creating an overflowing sales pipeline filled with their ideal clients at various stages of closure, ensuring a steady stream of new business.

RJ is the head of business development for a risk management firm. He regularly brings in new vital accounts. RJ has built a robust network of current and past clients, industry peers, and influencers who help him to identify new business opportunities for his firm. He has an established sales pipeline with opportunities at various stages. He converts 40% of his opportunities into a new business generating $5 million per year in revenues.

What Is Customer Centric?

Rain makers are customer centric; the customer is at the center of their process in everything they do. They proactively share their insider knowledge of success factors and proposed valued added solution to help improve their client's condition and outcomes. They have an attitude of "I understand the business conditions, and I have codified my experience in your market and have distilled it into action programs designed to increase profits, reduce cost, and increase your productivity." The opposite to customer centric is traditional selling, "Let me tell you about my company, I know more than you and my job is telling you about my company so you can decide how and where to use our service."

There are six steps required to develop a customer centric approach:

Getting positioned in your target market
Packaging your expertise
Building your visibility through promotion
Exceeding client expectations
Leverage client relationships
Developing centers of influences

Getting Positioned in Your Target Market

You need an organized process to find an entry point in the minds of a prospective customer by developing a point of view and way of thinking about a prospective customer's needs, challenges, concerns, and what's important to them. An understanding precisely of what you are marketing and selling and who you are selling to is the foundation for positioning and establishing yourself in your market.

Packaging Your Expertise

Making the intangible tangible, by taking the hot button needs you have discovered about your target market and individual prospects, putting it into words verbally (value proposition) and in writing (website, brochure and service descriptions) to create crystal clear communications that prospective customers can fully understand about what you do and the types of value you deliver.

Building Visibility Through Promotion

Using promotion is to gain the attention of highly qualified prospective clients. For rain makers, promotion is about visibility and credibility; people like to do business with companies and people who are familiar to them. If you are invisible, nobody will be thinking of you, let alone call you. Getting new meetings and appointments with prospects and converting them into customers is a rain maker's number one priority.

This is achieved by exceeding prospective customers' expectations, along every step of your process, this is especially important if you are targeting an underserviced customer of a competitor.

Leverage Customer Relationships

The goal is to have 100 percent of your desired customers as full-time customers. You are their go-to person for all of their needs. Rain makers understand that expanding existing customer relationships is one of the most effective and efficient ways to grow, by creating cross-selling opportunities, obtaining referrals and introductions to maintain an overflowing sales pipeline.

Developing Centers of Influences

These are noncustomer referral sources who can provide quality new leads and introductions, that is, efficient ways to market and sell reducing labor intensity and saving time. Top rain makers build secure networks' non-client referral sources that provide information on targeted accounts and generate leads.

What are Today's Selling Challenges?

Buyers have more options, and demand for buying and selling of your products and services is more sophisticated than it ever has been before due to the changing buyer preferences, increasing competition, suppliers competing, and commoditization of products and services.

There are four key challenges that sellers face today:

- Changing buyer preferences
- Increased competition
- Suppliers competing against you
- Commoditisation

Changing Buyer Preferences

A lot of this has to do with the ever changing buyer preferences. Buyers have access to more information and become smarter primarily due to the Internet. The Internet has been around since the early 1990s, however, it didn't really take hold in business until the mid 2000s when it started to take the form that we see it today, and that is when the information pendulum started shifting toward the buyer.

> Example: In the mid 90s, when you wanted to book a trip, the first step was contacting a travel agent, who were the brokers with all of the information via computer terminals feeding into the airlines. They would search for the best fares, negotiate with the airlines, and your tickets would then be sent in the mail. Today, almost 40% of airline travel is booked directly online by the customer with the airline. Airlines have been able to reduce their distribution costs, but more importantly, customers have a choice.
>
> Despite these technological advances, travel agents have not disappeared, they instead become travel advisers delivering convenience, access, and hard-core expertise. Some have fashioned themselves as magazine editors for hire, who can identify obscure new destinations and food trends. Others have morphed into spiritual coaches and party planners for the ultra-elite. Unexpectedly, the Internet has helped them flourish. Many of these firms have carved out a country-specific niche, from Mongolia to the Maldives. Others have morphed into party planners for the ultra-elite.

Increased Competition

The competition seems to be increasing daily, thanks mainly to the proliferation of digital technology and online marketing, including insurance advice, accounting services, legal, and many more. As business-to-business sellers, the technology is both a challenge and an opportunity, I regularly advise my financial clients to build a proprietary marketing system and focus their business development strategies on their top 20 percent of clients producing 80 percent of revenues.

Suppliers Competing Against You

Once upon a time, insurance companies only created a product that was sold through a network of agencies and brokers. Today, insurance companies are investing millions of dollars building their marketing and sales platforms to enable them to sell direct to customers, instead of solely relying on broker and agent's channels. Similar to airlines, it's quicker and cheaper to acquire and process business online, particularly for consumer and small to medium enterprise marketplace (SME). This technology shift is changing the way people purchase, and this is a tremendous opportunity across many industries from insurance, banking, finance, as the bottom 80 percent, low value, and high transaction type business are becoming automated.

Commoditization

Occurs when buyers can buy the same product or service from different small or large businesses. Price is the only distinguishing factor in commoditized products because there is no significant difference in quality or in how consumers use these products. Because buyers have so many additional purchasing options that didn't exist until recently, it can be confusing. One of the reasons the marketplace is so crowded is the many businesses simply do not have a compelling story of differentiation, no formal marketing and selling processes. Many are still focused on the old of way selling.

Why You Need Rain makers

Instead of relying on ad-hoc and/or hard sales and marketing tactics of hunters such as cold calling, rain makers instead take a pro-active and strategic approach, engaging in tasks to continually build and leverage their networks and contacts.

Top rain makers do not market to strangers, which involves hard work with low success and high rejection rates. Robert Middleton refers to this as *affiliation marketing* keeping in touch with the current and past clients and expanding your networking online with LinkedIn and offline with networking, referrals, and centers of influences. Rain makers focus their marketing efforts on the top 20 percent of clients, that generate 80 percent of sales and revenues. They invest the required time to educate and provide assistance to shift these customers from traditional selling (farmers and hunters) with a clear distinction between sales and service.

To support and encourage rain makers, smart businesses build high performing teams around these core characteristics developing a competitive advantage and more importantly, differentiation among a crowded field of competitors. Top rain makers also understand the importance of relationship management and actively manage critical relationships with team members, clients, prospects, referral sources, and suppliers.

By focusing on the top 20 percent of customers, allows more professionals to spend more time with their best customers with more complex needs. When rain makers prospect, they make connections through people, they know who they want to reach, and they find a way to get to that person through a warm introduction.

By adopting a rain maker approach, as a sales leader, you no longer need to distinguish between hunters and farmers. Instead, you can build a sales and marketing team around factors such as industry, product, or service expertise.

I believe all service business can benefit from rain maker style selling. The reality today is that everybody must develop proactive marketing and sales capabilities, instead of relying on a few people doing things the old-fashioned way. There are simply too many choices, competitors, do it yourself platforms, and websites. The capabilities to compete effectively are different today, any service business regardless of size can create a rain making culture and enjoy competitive advantage in the marketplace over their competitors.

Case Study

I once advised to a privately held financial services firm who was struggling to grow organically. They had enjoyed rapid growth the past few years by acquisition, this long-established firm had a strong brand. The founding partners had retired and there was confusion amongst the leadership team on how to grow the business. When the founders were building the business (making rain), generating leads, building relationships, creating opportunities, they did not share their business knowledge with the next generation of leaders and no one was taught how to sell. Staff watched the rain makers do their magic in awe, the rain makers would say, "Oh, we don't sell; we make things happen." It took a lot of persuasion and training, and new people coming on board to convince the firm that it's okay to use the word selling.

Summary

A rain maker is a person who generates revenue and profits by bringing new business.

- Think of rain making as a metaphor for money, in selling this is the highest form of this new development and the business that can develop rain makers have a distinct competitive advantage to differentiate themselves in a crowded marketplace
- Rain makers are customer centric; with the needs of the customer at the center of their process.
- They proactively share their insider knowledge of success factors.
- By adopting a rain maker approach, as a sales leader, you no longer need to distinguish between hunters and farmers. Instead, you can build a sales and marketing team around factors such as industry, product, or service expertise.
- The reality today is that everybody must develop proactive marketing and sales capabilities, instead of relying on a few people doing things the old-fashioned way. There are simply too many choices, competitors, do it yourself platforms, and websites.

CHAPTER 2

Myths That Stall Promising Careers?

If a cat sits on a hot stove, that cat won't sit on a hot stove again. That cat won't sit on a cold stove either. That cat just doesn't like stoves.
—Mark Twain

Just like the cat that won't sit on a stove again, there are myths and false beliefs that many professionals hold about marketing and selling that are holding them back from reaching their full potential as rain makers.

The legendary Ben Feldman regarded as one of the greatest salesmen in the world, the equivalent of a Michael Jordan in selling. He was written up in the Guinness Book of World Records for his accomplishments. He was a high school drop-out who commenced his selling career as a ten dollar a week egg salesman and was rejected for a sales job because he failed the aptitude test. Ben made the record books by selling life insurance for over 52 years, his lifetime sales volume $1.5 billion, with one-third of his sales coming after he reached the age of 65.

The incredible part of Ben's career is that he achieved his success working in Liverpool, Ohio, a small town of just 13,000 people. Ben's secret, he mastered the basics, he was customer focused on helping them get what they needed and wanted. Ben was not born with these skills, the Feldman method according to his former manager Andrew Thomson, is mostly procedural—a step-by-step, well-planned, logically thought-out pattern for action leading to a sale that Ben learned from the experiences of others.

This chapter is about fear, regardless of where you are in your career, all professionals can make significant improvements in their capabilities, whether you have been in business five minutes or several years. As a sales leader, your job is to help your professionals bust these myths and false belief's by overcoming their fears real or imagined that may be holding them and turning these fears into action. Gary Keller refers to these myths and false beliefs as myth-understanding, I don't know if that's an official word. However, I think the phrase is appropriate. By being able to recognize these fears as a leader, you will be able to help your professionals identify and take the necessary action to overcome.

The Seven Myths

I have come across seven-common myth-understandings that hold professionals back from becoming top rain makers:

Myth one:	I am not a natural born salespeople.
Truth:	Salespeople are made and not born.
Myth two:	I can't find the time for selling.
Truth:	You are probably trying to treat all of your clients equally.
Myth three:	I don't have the right knowledge.
Truth:	You know more than you think.
Myth four:	My clients don't want to deal with a salesperson.
Truth:	Your clients want you to be successful.
Myth five:	I am not an extravert.
Truth:	There is no evidence that extraverts sell more.
Myth six:	I am an introvert.
Truth:	Many of the world's top salespeople are introverts.
Myth seven:	I don't know anyone.
Truth:	You know more than you realize.

Myth One

Myth:	I am not a natural born salespeople.
Truth:	Great Salespeople are not born; they are made.

When you hear the word salesperson, what image comes to your mind? Whenever individuals are asked this question, the top five responses are usually, used car salesman, the man in a suit, insurance salesman, real estate agent, and pushy. Dan Pink says, "There are no 'natural' salespeople, in part because we're all naturally salespeople. I agree 100 percent, each of us because we're human has a selling instinct, we were born with it." This means that anyone can master the basics of moving others. Our beliefs about selling are often founded on outdated practices.

When I was growing up in California, in my neighborhood, there was a local Fuller Brush salesman who sold door-to-door; we also had the Avon Lady and Tupper wear parties. All these people were selling, as far I know, they made a good living from it and appeared to be enjoying themselves.

The good news is great salespeople are not born; they are made, selling is a skill, like running or public speaking that can be learned and mastered. As a leader, you can help displace this fear by having your house in order, for example, a clearly defined and branded selling process that helps guide professionals and provides step by a step training system that is clearly understood and used across the whole business.

This alone can help displace the fear with confidence. There are a few core traits successful rain maker's process, such as empathy, persistence, and emotional intelligence, meaning they are able to do this more naturally than most people.

Serena and Venus Williams were blessed with good eye and hand coordination, however, they still needed to be trained and continue to be coached today to achieve the full potential. There is no such thing as a natural born salespeople; all of the skills' capabilities required can be taught and learned through practice, coaching, and taking action.

Myth Two

Myth: I don't have the time for selling.
Truth: You have priorities and you are probably trying to treat all of your clients equally.

It's easy for professionals to fall into the service trap, especially as your customer portfolio grows. I have found professionals who struggle with time because there is misunderstanding regarding their roles and duties. When you try to treat all of your customers equally, you wind up providing "A" class service to "C" clients. The odd thing is that many of your bottom 80 percent of customers that contribute less than 20 percent of your revenue totals can take up over 50 percent of your time. Many of these tasks and requests can and should be handled by someone else.

An essential foundation to better managing time is ensuring and maintaining a clear division between sales and service. Begin by segmenting your clients, I see far too many professionals (farmers) trying to juggle 300 plus client relationships—they wind up becoming reactive instead of pro-active in managing their client relationships.

Better delegation of your lower value clients will dramatically increase the amount of time available for selling and marketing. Salespeople should sell, and service people should service, and top rain makers delegate work to the farmers.

In my work with financial services organizations, when there is a clear division between sales and service, everyone understands their roles, and professionals can focus the majority of their time on the critical functions of sales, customer retention, relationship management, and pipeline building who delegate routine work to support staff and team members generate more revenue; this happens because professionals—and their staff—can provide more time and services to clients, allowing the team to attract a wealthier clientele that demands more in-depth assistance.

So instead of increasing the number of clients per advisors, teams go *upmarket* with each client generating higher fees. I have several professional clients managing million-dollar portfolios, overseeing as many as 500 client relationships. These professionals delegate 80 percent of their work often consisting of the back of office work that does not require their attention. This means they only need to look after the top 20 percent of clients (40 to 75 key relationships) that are responsible for the bulk (up to 80%) of their revenues.

As a guide, 80 percent of a rain maker's day should be focused on sales-related activities including getting results for customers, getting results for your business, obtaining referrals, building and strengthening relationships with existing clients and replicating your best customers.

Every professional, as you will learn as we work through this book, can better allocate portions of their day for marketing related activities, even during those times when being pulled by client demands or other parts of the business. Selling is something that everyone can do and should do. And the solution for "I'm too busy to sell is to make marketing and selling a priority by scheduling it on the calendar.

Myth Three

Myth: I don't have the right knowledge?
Truth: You actually know more than you think.

John Savage once said, to be successful in selling follow the 95/5 rule, 95 percent people skills and 5 percent product knowledge, however, the real secret is learning as close to 100 percent of that 5 percent of product knowledge as possible.

Most professionals already process more than enough product knowledge to handle and answer 95 percent of customers questions. What is often is missing is knowing how to package your smarts to better attract prospective customers and that's probably the reason why reading this book, you want to be able to differentiate yourself, and there's no better way to differentiate yourself as being able to market and sell your expertise by packaging knowledge to meet your client's needs, this will be covered in chapter five.

Breaking the Rock

The San Antonio Spurs NBA basketball team one of the most successful sporting franchises in the world with five NBA championships and 22 straight playoff experiences. They have a saying at the San Antonio Spurs, "Breaking the Rock" that is each day they swing that sledgehammer and just whack the Rock it will slowly chip away. The 1 percent solution says improved by 1 percent per day in 70 days is twice as right. It's the same as breaking the rock principle is that each day you go in and just had a little bit more of that Rock, a little bit more. That Rock is your smarts and knowledge, being the becoming an excellent salesperson takes as long as it's going to take. Applying yourself each day top salespeople are continuously hone and perfect their skill.

Myth *Four*

Myth: My customers don't want to deal with a salesperson.
Truth: Your customers like doing business with successful people.

Genuine customers don't want to be sold to; however, they enjoy doing business with people they know, trust, and respect. Your customers have problems that require products, services, and solutions that your company provides. Your customer loyalty lies with your ability and the capabilities of your firm to get the job done, to meet their needs, to help them achieve their objectives. If you don't process adequate skills, they miss the opportunities to improve, and you miss out on future revenues. This why you owe it to yourself and business to develop persuasion skills.

Early on in my selling career in the insurance industry selling corporate insurance, I identified a gap in a existing client's business insurance program to protect their key executives. I carefully outlined the features and benefits and provided claim case examples for the CEO, who was hesitant to spend any more money on their risk program.

We had a good relationship, and over time, I provided additional information to educated him. He also conducted his own research. He finally agreed to purchase the additional coverage, and a few weeks later, they had a major event and if they didn't have that coverage in place, the company would have been in serious financial trouble. My client thanked me for being persistent.

I have always believed if a customer has a strong need and you have the products and services to address this need, then you owe it to yourself, your customer, and your business to make sure that you have the skills and capabilities to address your client's needs adequately. That's less about being a salesperson and more about looking after your customer's best interest.

Myth *Five*

Myth: What if I am not an extrovert?
Truth: There is no evidence to support that extroverts are
               better sales people.

The extrovert and introvert personality types are actually a kind of spectrum, extreme extroverts fall on one end and extreme introverts fall on the other and most people end somewhere in the middle. An extrovert is someone who enjoys being around people; comfortable in social situations and assertive. This type of person sounds like the ideal salesperson; however, there is no evidence to supports this. Researchers have investigated the relationship between extroversion and sales success, and they have found the link to be flimsy at best. Non extroverts may feel that they are not cut-out for sales because they don't have the gift of the gab. Extroverts may tend to have an easier time connecting prospects and building rapport, and don't mind spending time cold calling.

Myth Six

Myth:	What if I am an introvert?
Truth:	Introverts are just as effective as extraverts in selling.

Introverts are often thought of as quite reserved and thoughtful individuals who don't seek special attention or social engagements. There is zero evidence supporting a correlation between extroversion and sales performance. A Harvard Business Review reports that showy type salespeople are more likely to alienate prospects then close them and salespeople in the top 90 percent demonstrate traits of modesty and humility.

Ben Feldman mentioned at the beginning of this chapter was a shy, softly spoken, and very humble gentlemen. Successful rain makers come in all shapes, sizes, and personality types. According to author Dan Pink, the ideal sales professionals are ambiverts, a person who has a balance of extrovert and introvert features in their personality, they are flexible and able to use their heads and heart. When searching for rain makers, it's a mistake to overlook someone because they are quiet and reserved the key trait you should be looking for is someone with empathy.

Myth Seven

Myth:	What if I don't know anyone?
Truth:	You actually no more people than you realize, you; probably just need to organize your contact information.

As a professional, you know more people than you probably realize, however, your list of names is probably not organized, for example, LinkedIn ties in with the old concept of six degrees of separation, which is grounded in the idea that any person in the world is linked with any other person by no more than six people. Increasing the size of your network is one the secrets of the success of top rain makers, which we will cover in a later chapter. Successful rain makers have been using this concept for years, and LinkedIn has made it more accessible. According to researchers, the average American knows about 600 people. By building your contact list of everyone you know and then using LinkedIn to connect is a good place to start.

Case Study

CJ was as a sales executive with an advertising firm. New business development had always been a struggle and his superior was concerned about his performance. I spent a day in the field with CJ accompanying him on several calls. I noticed on the first few calls that he was nervous and did not appear confident.

It turned out this was CJ's first sales job. He thought as a salesperson he needed to be a fast talker and an extrovert, and he was neither. During the next few sales calls, I had CJ write out his beliefs about the product he was selling and its benefits for customers. I instructed him before each call to read the card and to speak and simply focus and have a conversation about the customer needs. He was less nervous and closed a sale on his last appointment of the day. His firm continued to work with him, and CJ developed into a reliable salesperson for his company, regularly exceeding his monthly sales target.

Summary

- As a sales leader, your job is to help your professional bust these myths and false beliefs, and translate fear into action.
- There are seven-common myth-understandings that hold professionals back from becoming top rain makers.

CHAPTER 3

How 21st Century Rain makers Think and Act?

Top sales luminaries cannot consciously describe how they perform their own sales magic.

—Dr Donald Moine

All marketing and selling skills are learnable, and I believe, any professional can sharpen their skills; naturally, some will develop into better salespeople than others and skill level will vary from high to low just as they do in all professions.

A recruiter once told me there is one constant demand from his business clients, to find someone to sell their products and services, they want a natural born salespeople. Numerous tests have been devised to unearth sales abilities. Unfortunately, as most employers have discovered, the born salesperson is a myth no such person exists.

The simple fact is outstanding salespeople are made—developed—not born. Selling is an acquired skill, and one that can be developed to some degrees by anyone. Top professionals develop and hone their skills through diligent study and practice on the fundamental techniques.

I have observed from working with and coaching top professionals seven ways to think and act:

Concept mindset
Think big goals
Focused
Think process
Deep motivation
Optimistic
Action oriented

What Is a Concept Mindset?

Top professionals understand that sales performance starts with you and your philosophy of selling. The kind of person you are, your ambitions, your motives, and ethics. Everyone already has a philosophy whether they are aware of it or not; your attitude and beliefs determine this toward selling. Your happiness and success in selling should stand upon a sound philosophy of sale; this is so fundamental and important when you combine skill in marketing with a deep-seated belief in the benefits of your offering that you have the unbeatable combination.

A sound philosophy is not only true for top sales professionals but for great leaders of history were those with strong convictions that cause was right with the ability to persuade others to follow them, such as, Winston Churchill, Martin Luther King, Abraham Lincoln are examples of the power created by combining sales ability with conviction.

Your sales philosophy impacts your integrity and work ethics. Professionals with poor work ethics are often lying to themselves by playing games, motived and doing the work required to be successful, in reality, they are afraid and procrastinating. This has a flow on effect, over promising, under delivering, or worse, lying to customers and prospects—a road that leads to nowhere.

A well thought out sales philosophy helps rain makers to become fearless in their marketing and selling. Developing your sales philosophy begins with understanding your "Big Why" clarifying the kind of person you are, your ambitions, motives, and ethics.

Your sales philosophy and integrity are closely linked. Begin examining your philosophy, by asking yourself these two questions:

On September 11, 2001, DK an insurance executive life changed. His best friend never made it home that night. The man "didn't have a life insurance agent. Didn't have a financial adviser. Didn't have an estate attorney or anything like that," DK said. "He had very little protection for his family." His friend knew he needed to fix that. But he ran out of time, and his family left without protection coverage when he died unexpectedly. What happened to his family was a tragedy, DK made the decision immediately that he was going to focus the rest of his career on making sure there are fewer people like that tomorrow than there are today. It has culminated in DK's sales philosophy that has helped him guide one of the largest life insurers in the United States.

Do you see selling as a high calling requiring a great degree of skill, knowledge, character, and integrity?

Or do you see it as a way to make money quickly—with no holds barred on any tactics, justified as long as you make a sale?

Your "Big Why"

Defines and helps you to remain the focused on your concept. Professionals who understand their "Big Why" and concept focus usually outperform those who are solely product focused. They are customer centered, obtaining more repeat business, and higher retention rates because they take the long view with their customers. Your "Big Why" is critical when establishing your goals both personally and professionally.

Think Big Goals

Top performers understand the power of setting goals, they think big, as opposed to small, overly cautious, hesitant. Little plans lack the magic that stirs the blood. They are thrilled by the chance of testing themselves with a long stretch on a limb.

There are two types of goals—personal and professional. Our focus is your professional production goals you set for yourself and career. Yearly goals will never be reached without the setting of achieving short-term goals.

Rain maker live and sell on a day-to-day basis; they know what needs accomplishing on a short-term basis as well. Reaching a yearly goal is reaching a series of weekly and monthly goals. Top performers understand the importance of the power of setting big goals to their goals and work backwards to build good solid habits to achieve them. As you place your goals, you need to establish practices to reach them.

Top professionals do all those necessary things to achieve success, including getting rid of procrastination, distractions, and whatever is preventing them from controlling themselves. Self-discipline is being a self-starter and taking charge of yourself, developing the right attitude, including taking responsibility for their learning and development rising, enabling them to serve their clients better.

Great habits lead the big goals to help you to grow into your goals. The goals that I am referring to are your production goals to propel your career. There are different types of goals, physical, personal, family, and so forth. These are all important, and all top professionals should have them. Goal setting will be covered thoroughly in Chapter 11.

Seven Professional Goal Categories

Focus
New Customers
Retention
Revenue
Prospects
New customers
Average revenue per customer
Prospect quality

Focus

By creating groups, your goals tracking become simpler and highly focused. You simply run down the list and fill in the blanks; this is the most effective and efficient way to set goals and to focus your attention and efforts of those areas that will impact your businesses. Goal categories act as placeholders that need your attention; everyone needs to understand how their numbers work

New Customers

New customers are essential; it's easy to fall into the trap of thinking that selling more to existing clients is more than adequate to drive growth.

The reality is clients move on, retire, go out of business, circumstances change, and so forth. So you need to continually broaden your base with new clients each year continually. Set a goal to surpass the previous new customers results.

Retention

Retention includes the total income a customer generates. If your average revenue per customer is $1,000 and in the following year, there's a reduction in pricing by 10 percent, you retain the same number of customers your retention rate has reduced from 100 to 90 percent, and your revenue has also decreased by 10 percent. Ultimately, your retention goal should be 100 percent of your desired customers.

Average Revenue Per Customers

There are only three ways to increase your revenue: first by increasing the average size of each sale, second acquiring larger customers, and third, by selling more to your existing customers.

Prospect Quality

Your sales pipeline is an indicator of future business success; you should establish goals for each stage, including lead generation, presentations and closing to ensure you maintain an overflowing pipeline. If your retention goal is to keep 100 percent of your desired clients, then 80 percent of your annual sales budget is already achieved, so your sales pipeline goal should be to have 30 percent growth to guarantee the other 20 percent. When this happens, selling becomes fun.

Client Development

To achieve 100 percent retention, you need full-time customers. For the top 20 percent of customers, you are their number one and only source; your goals, 100 percent of your top 20 percent of customers are full-time.

Referrals

There are two types of referrals, unsolicited and pro-active. With the former, your customers provide you with names and introductions and the latter you educate and ask your top customers for names and introductions. Referrals are a vast untapped source for new business that many professionals under-utilize.

Professional Development

A professional career does not standstill. As you establish your goals, ask yourself, what new information and habits do I need to learn to support my goals? Professional development should be continuous, including conferences, books, seminars, workshops to keep up. Doctors, lawyers, and accountants are required to undergo professional development to keep up with new advances and legislation changes. The same should apply within the profession of selling.

Ben Feldman's success came down to having a straightforward goal formula of just three sales per week. His goal never changed. What did change, however, was the value of those three sales each week, to where they were worth millions of dollars. Even up to the last days of his career, he worked well into his 80's. Ben's goal was still three sales per week. Top performers establish their goals and break them down; this gives them the platform to set their planning for the year.

What About Focus?

John Savage once said, "Work eight hours, sleep eight hours, just make sure it's not the same eight hours." What he meant was, when you leave home to go to work, try doing it. Focus is about understanding and implementing your "Big Why" the way you do the things that you do.

Become concept focused, role as a rain maker is a means to an end to help your clients achieve their objectives. Understanding your purpose leads to clarity and focus making it easier to prioritize your time, resources balancing your career, and personal life. Successful salespeople often seem to make everything look effortless, while average performers around them are working 60 to 70 hours per week just to keep their head above water. Top performers are very clear about their reasons "why" this is what fuels their success.

Think Process

Top performers early in their careers adopt a *fake it until you make it* mentality through practice, hard works of producing results acquired an impossible to fail mentality. When I was just starting out in my financial services career, working for an international insurance company, the first time I was presented (told) of my sales target, I thought there was no way I was ever going achieve it. However, once the goal was set (in my case, it was handed to me), I acted fearlessly, and things started to come into play, and developing the right habits, I grew into the goal.

As I sought help from more experienced professionals, asked lots of questions and focused my efforts, it was not long before I became very efficient at recognizing new business opportunities, retaining 100 percent of my key accounts and successfully upselling existing clients. The result, I exceeded my initial unachievable budget by 20 percent and continued to do so for the next several years.

Top rain makers develop their impossible to fail attitude by creating sales processes for the types of business for the ideal clients. By trusting their process, they understand if they follow it, the results will take care of themselves.

What About Motivation?

Becoming a successful rain maker is not complicated, but it is difficult. To execute your plans every day, you must have a deep level of motivation to fuel the process. Successful rain makers make themselves execute the fundamentals, while the less successful cannot. And having a sustained level of motivation is essential. It starts with establishing the right goals and working in milestones. Ben Feldman broke his goals down to just three sales per week; this was simple and easy to follow; it helped keep him motivated toward his goals each week and the related task.

Using your sales process to track exactly where prospective clients are at each stage and help motivate you to move them from one step to the next in your pipeline and eventually to convert them into new clients and revenue. Each step becomes a mini goal to achieving your main goals.

I regularly work out in the gym several days a week (I used to be a competitive powerlifter), now I just compete with myself "can I go a couple of pounds heavier on the bench press than I did last week?" These mini goals help me to keep my workouts exciting and productive. It allows me to set my own goals and the motivation to achieve them. Top rain makers trust their process and focus on focusing them on the milestones to stay motivated.

What About Action?

The very best gamify (not sure this is an actual word) their business task to turn business development activities into a game to make it more exciting or enjoyable. Rain makers are action oriented; they set business and activity goals and track their process, developing the motivation to fuel their process and action to turn their plans into reality, with regular practice, these become habits.

Jerry Seinfeld, one of the world's most successful comedians, learned early in his career how to gamify the task of writing jokes (a vital tool for a comedian) to beat procrastination using a big calendar he hung on a prominent wall. Every day Jerry wrote a joke, he'd put an x through that day, the days turned into a few weeks, and finally, a chain of days of x's on his calendar that he refused to break. Gamifying, his works allowed Seinfeld to create thousands of jokes that he uses regularly to entertain audiences

Lack of Action is the number one thing that prevented hardworking professionals developing promising careers. They set their goals, developed sales plans that outline they must see x number of people per day to achieve their goal, but they never take action, by doing a little bit each day. For example, identifying a certain amount of new names every day to add to their prospect list.

Professionals who fail to obtain new names each day don't because they are unable to think about it. The cure is to devise a plan and gamify it that will not permit you to forget to do it. Doing a little bit of marketing daily, sometimes 15, 20, 30 minutes a day, is a lot better than trying to do three, four, or five hours a day or work in a crisis mode.

What About Optimism?

There is a famous joke about a child who wakes up on Christmas morning surprised to find a heap of horse manure under the tree instead of a collection of presents. Yet, the child is not discouraged because he has an extraordinarily optimistic outlook on life. His parents find him enthusiastically shoveling the manure as he exclaims, "With all this manure, there must be a pony somewhere!" Selling is hard work. It's one of the most challenging jobs in the world. You face continual rejection, potential failure, and persistent disappointment, setbacks, obstacles, and difficulties that are not experienced by most people.

Rain makers are optimistic; they understand the reality that selling is not easy; it has never been easy; it will never be easy, however, your attitude will ultimately account for a large part of your success. It's the outward expression of everything you are. A positive attitude toward life and the inevitable ups and downs is a trait that successful rain makers share. If you ask for a referral, what's the worst thing going to happen?

Your scheduled meeting with a prospective client does not go to plan, or worst still they cancel. How do you think when bad things happen? When this does happen, and in selling, it will, the pessimist thinks, "It's all my fault" even when there is nothing they could have done to change the outcome. Optimists, on the other hand, think when bad things happen that they are not accountable for all of it and while it might ruin their day, it won't ruin their life. They isolate the ill effects. When good things happen, the pessimist says, "I had nothing to do with it", the Optimist on the other hand says, I caused it. The pessimist says, "It won't last", the Optimist says "It's going to last forever".

Marshall Goldsmith writes: "Optimism [is] not only feeling it inside but showing it on the outside—a magic move. People are automatically drawn to a confident individual who believes everything will work out."

Some people are born with a deep-seated optimism personality trait. Some are an overly optimistic assessment of their abilities in areas where they lacked expertise can cause difficulty. Confidence is a skill, and many people can become more optimistic, and most people can learn enough to succeed in sales.

Case Study

Billy was in a sales slump, he asked for me to spend the day observing and provide some feedback to help improve his performance. Billy scheduled seven appointments, five with existing customers and two with prospective customers. The first two meetings with existing customers did not go well. I spoke to Billy about his "Big Why" (sales concept) he had not given this any thought, he just knows that he was supposed to sell. I asked him a few questions about his motivations, ethics, and beliefs on the positive outcomes of his services.

We turned his answers into his selling concepts. He copied this onto a 3 × 5 card that he kept in the briefcase. For the rest of the day, before each call, I suggested he reads his sales concept before each meeting to remind him of the great value he provides for his customers. I told him, "Some days clients will rain on your parade", and your sales philosophy will keep you grounded. The great success is the rest of the day, even picking up a new customer. Billy went on to become a solid performer for his firm, consistently exceeding his growth targets.

Summary

- All the marketing and selling skills are learnable.
- Seven key traits and characteristics of successful salespeople process:
  - Think concept
  - Think big goals
  - Think focus
  - Think process
  - Think motivation
  - Think optimism
  - Think action

PART II

The Four Frameworks

The Four Fundamental Frameworks
for Rain maker Success

From all of my experience and research, four frameworks stand out as foundations for a highly successful career as a rain maker. Following these frameworks should help you put your professionals on the surest and quickest path to sales achievement. We will walk through each of these frameworks and explain what you will need to apply these frameworks at a high level.

To be highly successful as a rain maker, it is important that you understand that you need to think like a businessperson. Frameworks are about action. These four frameworks represents the four major areas in which you must take effective action to develop your professionals into effective rain makers.

CHAPTER 4

What's Your Service Framework?

The first step in service marketing is your service.

—Harry Beckwith

The first framework is your client service focusing on the strategies and behaviors that affect the delivery, support and ultimately the retention of your desired clients.

Top rain makers do not work in isolation; they rely on and leverage the skills, talent, and resources to maximize their efficiency allowing them to focus their time and energy on the right type of activities to produce continued new business growth. A service framework ensures there's a strong division between sales and service. Top performers operate on the belief that salespeople should sell, and service people should service.

It's too easy for professionals to fall into the service trap, they often start with the best of intentions, but get caught up spending too much time servicing existing clients unable to distinguish between selling and servicing.

Without a clear distinction, a professional's new business production will plateau as they become a highly paid customer service representatives saying, "I am too busy to go out and sell." excuse and hiding behind activities, due to lack of accountability, fear and lack of clarity. Results, no sales pipeline, relationships and poor retention of key accounts.

The Three Key Elements of You Service Framework

There are four key areas to your service framework, first there is responsive teamwork, second, creating a continuation process for existing customers, third, workflow management to standardize repetitive operations and expertise.

What is Responsive Teamwork?

Everyone associated with your business recognizes and is committed to the marketing activities and everything associated as a vital core function of the way things are done in the business, one of your competitive advantages. Outstanding customer centered teams are focused on the customer's needs and use their knowledge capabilities to deliver value on time, every time and within budget that leads to long-term retention of desirable clients, builds value-based relationships with key players, and makes superior performance that leads to client satisfaction the driving force in your business. Teamwork is required for maintaining a strong division between sales and service allowing rain makers to focus on selling and building relationships. Your client service framework ensures the right behaviors and strategies to maximize your professionals' time and resources.

Top rain makers are 80 percent externally focused and only 20 percent internally externally.

The opposite is true of less effective rain makers, who focus 80 percent of their time and energy on internal activities and just 20 percent on external, resulting in the I am too busy to sell scenario. Your service model makes it easier for professionals to focus on their key relationships by, delegating routine and transactional work to others on the team.

80/20 Focus

Professionals should be focusing on, attracting prospective clients, retaining existing key accounts (top 20 percent), achieving overall sales results and generating referrals to prospective clients. The 80/20 rule also known as Pareto's Principle. Vilfredo Pareto was an Italian economist and sociologist in the late 1800s, the 80/20 Rule evolved from a study of land ownership. Pareto discovered that 20 percent of the people owned 80 percent of the land and vice versa. Pareto determined that there was a predictable imbalance in the universe that stemmed from the 80/20 Rule. Since then, this principle has been applied to almost every aspect of life, including personal happiness (20% of what you do gives you 80% of your joy in life). The bottom line is that 80 percent of consequences/results come from 20 percent of the causes/ activities.

The 80/20 Rule applies in most businesses, the top 20 percent of clients generate 80 percent of revenue and the bottom 80 percent of clients generate 20 percent of revenues.

Over the years, I have found some additional predictable imbalances in businesses. For example:

The Top 5% of customers = 50% of revenue (Your "A" customers)

The Middle 15% of customers = 30% of revenue (Your "B" customers)

The Bottom 80% of customers = 20% of revenue (Your "C" customers)

The bottom 50% of customers only generate about 5% of the revenue and that the bottom 25% generate even less—about 2% of the revenues.

Conversely, the "Mega A" customers (the top 2%) bring in roughly 35 percent of the revenue.

Following the 80/20 rule:

List your customers from largest to smallest by revenue and categorize every client as follows:

Category A—top 5%

Category B—middle 15%

Category C—bottom 80%

Rain maker should focus on the top 20 percent accounts (Category A and B), with the service teams handling the bottom 80 percent, this will allow your service people to do what they do best, looking after the day-to-day needs of the clients and improve their own capabilities.

Assign marketing responsibility by level of responsibility for example:

Staff—Develop sound relationships at assigned levels and identify additional needs. Develop relationships at right levels, presell needs for additional services, contribute to referrals, and make results visible.

I was working with an insurance business struggling to grow organically; I quickly discovered the problem, all the professionals were spending 90% of their time on day-to-day client issues, many of which could easily be solved by customer staff. The group of 20 professional were each trying to manage between 300 to 400 accounts and were too busy to try to find new business. The service people were bored and frustrated because as they had nothing to do, with the only routine work being delegated they were not developing their professional skills, resulting in a constant turnover of support staff and frustrated professionals, which had a negative impact on client retention.

Rain maker and leadership—Capitalize on needs, develop referrals, widen relationships, determine sources of new clients and capitalize on new opportunities.

What Is Client Continuation?

Client continuation is the second part of the service framework. This is a customer centric marketing program for the continual building and strengthening of you desired client relationships. It's far too easy to become complacent about a client's loyalty; this is especially true when he is only required to make a crucial purchase decision annually, such as renewing a lease, subscription, or insurance agreement. Client continuation is a five-stage process:

Engage—During the engagement phase, you create customer service plans, identify need problems, and opportunities.

Enter—The core strategy is to manage the customer expectations, develop service level agreements, and developing the account management plan.

Deliver—While every process is different, your goal is to manage visibility, and provide the agreed solutions (product and services).

Follow up—The goal is customer satisfaction, stewardship reporting to the client to demonstrate the value provided "This is what we promised, and this is what we have delivered" preselling any additional needs and solutions that you have identified.

Support—The most important factor to bring items of interest to the client and asking for referrals and introductions. A robust continuation process will help you build and maintain breakthrough relationships with your key customers. It's important to note that a continuous process is not intended for every customer, that would be too time-consuming. Instead, use the 80/20 rule and categorize each customers into A-B-C categories.

Focus on the top 20 percent of customers generating 80 percent of revenues. The goal, 100 percent retention of top 20 percent of key and desired clients producing the bulk of your revenues.

A solid continuation process details your client journey from lead generation right through to the delivery of their service and stewardship and everything in between. The number of steps is not important as this will vary according to your business, products, services, and markets that you serve. When you combine your continuation process with your brand, you will have a unique selling system.

Your continuation process is also the ideal way to train and develop staff and delegate tasks and activities freeing up professional's time to focus on rain making money-making activities of building relationships and building their sales pipelines. The best continuously develops their client service framework to ensure that it's continually meeting the needs of their business.

Begin developing your client continuation process:

- Make a list your category "A" customers.
- Outline the steps on how they became a customer.
- Create a map, visual that outlines each of these steps.
- Identify areas where you can add value to your process that differentiates you.

What Is Account Rounding?

Account rounding up is providing additional value to your existing clients. Every business has important accounts, where they can and should be doing more business, I refer to these as part-time clients. They may have additional needs that have not been fully explored or are being met by another competitor. Either way part-time customers are a risk; first, you are leaving money/revenue left on the table and secondly, you created an opening for a competitor to offer additional services.

The benefits of a customer continuation process is that part-time clients are easily identified and plans can be developed for converting these to full-time clients. Implementing a customer service framework leaves nothing to chance. The goal all of your desired clients into 100 percent fulltime clients.

What Is Workflow Management?

Every workflow, model, and process needs to be documented. Proper workflow management is critical, and it's also the ideal way to train and develop staff and upgrade capabilities across your whole firm. I know of a business that lost a critical account because a key person was away and no one else was able to understand how to process or transact a piece of business and the customer went elsewhere. A sound workflow management system prevents this from happening, saving valuable time. It enables things to get done quicker and faster and allowing professionals to quickly hand over day-to-day customer routine work on top clients, to ensure that it gets done.

What Is Workflow Automation?

Time is often wasted due to poor and inefficient handling of information. Automation includes paperless processing, electronic filing, scanning, electronic file organization, and contact management. Automation today is essential, and the technology available is inexpensive, making it very easy and cost-effective to have everyone using automation at least 80 percent of the time. Services including Sharepoint, Google Docs, Microsoft's OneNote, Evernote, and Dropbox, allow you to keep all your intellectual property and information libraries, client proposals, engagement toolkits, proposals, sales processes, and checklist in a handy location making it easy for everyone to access using the cloud, and knowing how to access the information quickly can be a tremendous benefit.

Case Study

I was assisting a company to improve organic growth. The CEO said, "We've invested a lot of money on getting quality salespeople, this investment has not translated into growth." I quickly found the problem, all of their salespeople were busy servicing existing customers instead of looking for new ones. They believe their clients only wanted to deal with them, and they were afraid to let the service go and have the service team manage the day-to-day issues. Working with the CEO, we segmented their clients, reducing their client workload by 75 percent. The reduced workload allowed them to spend the majority of their time on sales-related activities, and this became the new normal and business grew.

Summary

- Client service model focusing on the strategies and behaviors that affect your service team.
- Top rain makers do not work in isolations; they rely on and leverage the skills and talents of support people to maximize their efficiency to focus on the right things to ensure continued business growth.
- A Client Service Framework consists of: Teamwork, continuation process, rounding out of accounts, and work flow management.

CHAPTER 5

What Is Your Sales Framework?

Many remain unskilled by finding fault with their tools
—Gerard Nierenberg

Every business consists of three elements, products, services, and relationships. Products are tangible purchases such as a car, television, or book. Services are intangible purchases, such as a warranty, membership or advice. Relationships are intangible purchases that are on trust, your brand, image, and reputation.

Rain makers understand their products and services are commodities where price is often the determining factor. They focus on ensuring their products and services are competitive enough to meet the needs of their markets, and instead focus the bulk of their time and energy on developing superior relationships that provide a competitive advantage, which is not easily duplicated by competitors.

Your sales framework is about the activities required to produce breakthrough relationships that ultimately drive new business growth. Developing professionals into rain makers is a series of steps that build on one another. Developing good habits early, dramatically increases this process whilst significantly reduces the time required to get there. Taking proper steps in the beginning is the fastest and easiest route to success.

The fundamentals don't change, for example, the Harlem Globetrotters basketball team have mastered the fundamentals of the game, passing, shooting, and doing layups and while they entertain the audience, however, they are still playing basketball.

The Three Key Elements of Your Sales Framework

First, there is market focus ensuring you focus your time in the right areas. Second, is your selling system your process to manage your existing relationships. Third, the marketing activities you engage in to build your network. Salespeople are not born; salespeople are made, and all the skills you need for sales success are learnable as long as you have the foundation, attitude, and mindsets.

What is Focus?

A rain maker's number one (in many cases the only) job is bringing in new revenue and prestige by managing the relationships of desired existing customers; they spend 80 percent of their available time concentrating on four key activities:

- Results—Instead of just being busy, before undertaking any activity, ask yourself, "Will this activity help with me with achieving my result or am I just being active and hiding behind actions?"
- Referrals—Generated from existing customers and centers of influence
- Retention—To retain 100 percent of your desirable customers
- Replication—Acquiring new customers that are clones of your best top 20 percent of customers who contribute 80 percent of revenues.

Focusing on these activities will simplify your selling process. Whenever I work with a business that is struggling with growth, I often find that people who are supposed to be responsible for business development spending the majority (up to 80%) of their time on service-related issues instead of sales-related activities.

What is Your Selling System?

A selling system is a formal sales process for identifying prospective customers and converting them into clients. Top performers have a structured sales process that is followed by everyone right across your business. A clear process has several advantages, first it becomes easier to attract and train professionals, second, it maintains a clear division between sales and service, and finally, it keeps track of prospects in the sales pipelines. A sales selling system consists of three parts as shown in Figure 5.1.

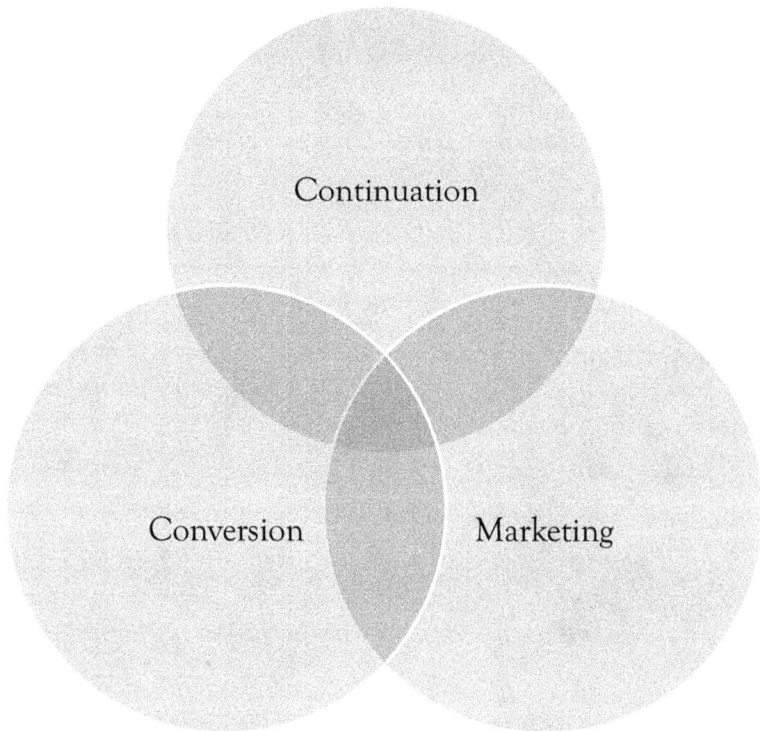

Figure 5.1 Sales process

Continuation Process

Continuation means, continuing the relationships instead of renewing business or assuming, this is a customer centric approach to manage and develop existing relationships. It's far too easy to take these relationships for granted, especially if someone has been doing business with you for a number of years. In some industries, such as insurance and accounting, professionals may only see their clients annually. The continuation process commences when you deliver your product or service. For an insurance professional, this is when the policy is delivered, or for an accountant when the tax returns are completed. This is when you should start tracking and implementing your plan.

The absence of a continuation program is a major reason why cross-selling is a struggle for so many.

Top professionals use a multidimensional approach, looking at the total relationship and creating a process to maximize the value for the

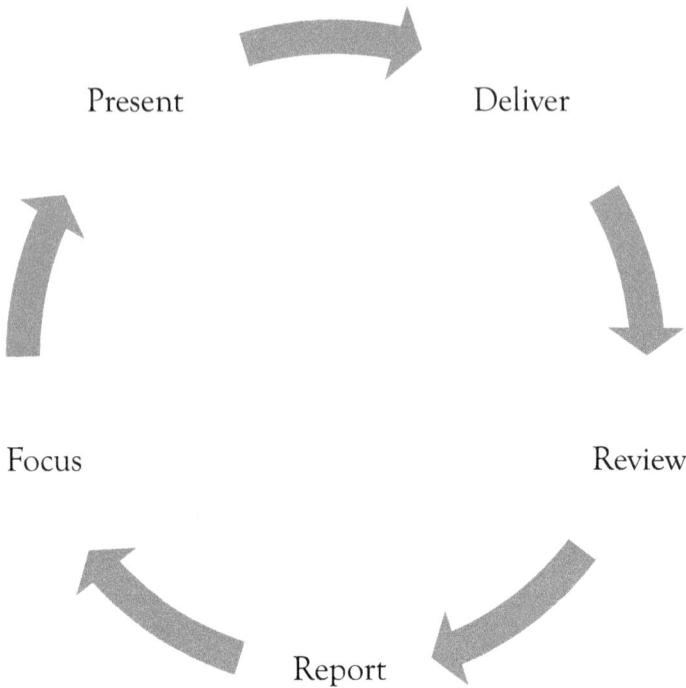

Figure 5.2 Continuation process

customer, which in turn maximizes retention and increases the customer lifetime value through referrals and introductions. Figure 5.2 is a sample continuous process for a services business.

Step 1—Deliver: This starts the process. Every service should have a personal delivery; this can be in person, by phone, or virtually. The goal is to provide VIP service for your desired customers.

Step 2—Review: This can be by phone, in person, newsletter to check up and educate your client.

Step 3—Report: This is an ideal opportunity to provide a stewardship report—letting the client know what's been achieved to date and remind the value that been delivered.

Step 4—Focus: Options include, in person, by phone, virtually review plans and update strategies.

Step 5—Pre: Negotiation, delivery, and renewal of services.

These five steps are a continuance loop that will help you to manage visibility of your key and desired customers. The number of steps you have is less important than having consistent process followed by everyone.

Your marketing process

These are the activities and steps you take to identify leads and eventually convert those leads into prospective customers. Figure 5.3 is a sample marketing process.

> Stage 1—Strangers: People who are unknown to you; however, they have the characteristics and traits of your ideal client profile.
> Step 2—Affiliates: You are connected through an affiliation such as past clients, club membership, LinkedIn connections (1st degree connection) and so on.

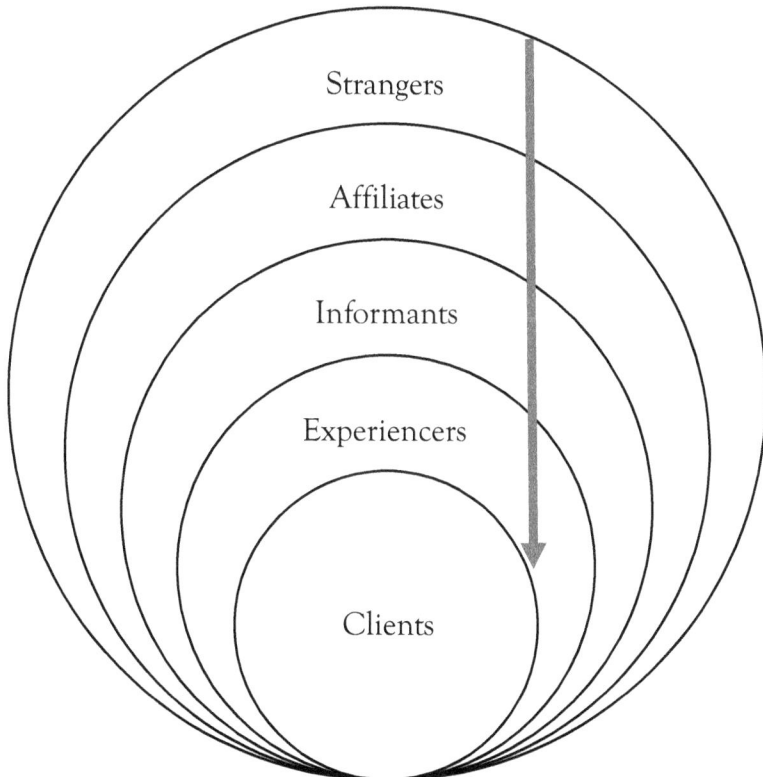

Figure 5.3 Marketing process

Step 3—Informants: They know who you are, have seen you around, are familiar with you through your blog post or attendance at conferences, read your articles or met you at a networking event.

Step 4—Experiencers: You are providing value through your newsletters, articles, blog post, webinars, and so forth. They have subscribed to some of your services.

Step 5—Clients: Your process should map out clearly how new opportunities flow through to the business and how you nurture leads and a prospective client who are merely not ready to buy yet to keep a steady stream of potential clients flowing into your sales pipeline and converting into new business.

New Business Process:

The third and final piece is your new business process. There are usually several steps a prospect goes through before they convert into customers. Each of these are connected, a new business prospect eventually will end up in your continuation process (see Figure 5.4).

Lead—Obtained through networking, referral or introduction.

Meeting—In person, virtually, or by phone to explore their needs.

Qualify—Asking questions to determine if the individual fits your ideal client profile, has a need that you can satisfy.

Present—Your products or solutions to meet their needs.

Objections—Addressing the prospects' questions or concerns.

Close—Successfully agree on price.

Referrals—Asking existing customers for names and introductions to prospective customers.

When this is working well, your sales time is dramatically reduced with the majority of business coming from referrals and introductions, that makes the whole process seamless, less labor intensive and more enjoyable. Your processes are guides that help you to identify and understand where you are in the process and the steps required to keep moving forward.

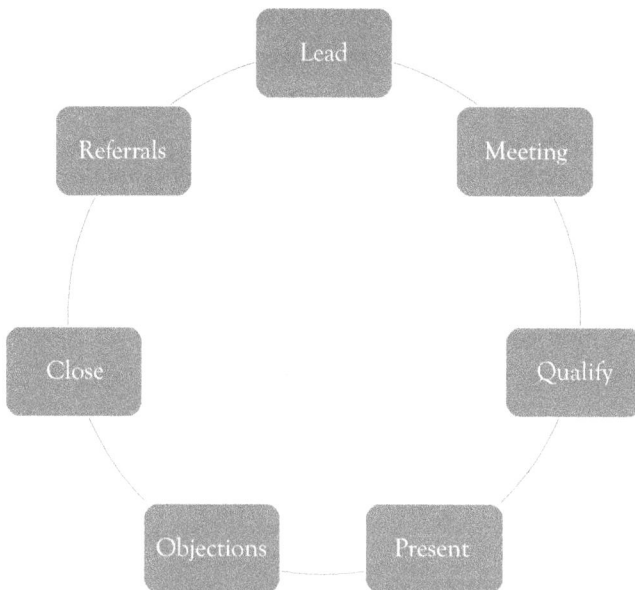

Figure 5.4 New business process

What Are Marketing Actvities?

Referral Marketing

The best generate 75 percent or more of their new business from referrals or introductions. However, it's not just any type of referrals, you want referrals that are clones of your very best clients. Obtaining referrals is a crucial sales capability that is also learnable, and makes selling more comfortable when a prospect comes to you.

In many cases, 50 percent of the hard work has already been done. Your top clients are your best referral sources; there are two types of referrals—solicited and unsolicited; there's needs to be an action plan in place to actively manage both types. One of the reasons why many professionals, both new and experienced, don't generate sufficient referrals is that they make the mistake of relying too heavily on unsolicited referrals because they are afraid to ask. In fear of upsetting their customer. Customer are more than happy provide referrals, but you have to help them to help you. Develop the habit of educating your customers to help them to help you. The very best proactively ask their top clients for referrals to maintain a full sales pipeline.

When the majority of your new business leads are via referral and introduction, your appointment conversion ratio will dramatically improve and new business generation will become cost-effective and more enjoyable.

Another excellent source of referrals is through centers of influences, develop between five-to-ten center of influences, nonclient referral sources that can help you identify, introduce and provide, good reliable referrals and introductions to your ideal customers.

If you meet your centers of influence quarterly, if you have ten and each provides you with three names per quarter, that equal to 120 new leads per years with little acquisition cost and stress. You should be able to obtain meetings with 50 percent of these leads putting you way ahead of your competitors.

Relationship Marketing

No one achieves success operating in a vacuum even if you are a solo business professional. Relationship marketing is an extension of your continuation process, as outlined in Figure 5.5. Rain makers nurture five critical relationships.

  Customer relationships—All clients are not created equally. Focus your marketing efforts on the 20 percent clients that generate 80 percent of your revenues. This is the primary focus on your continuation process, and every client in this category should have a formal plan in place.

  Colleagues—Rain makers do not work in isolation; they also managed their internal client relationships, which can include assistants and colleagues.

  Centers of influence—There are two sources for referrals, existing clients and nonclient sources—these are referred to as centers of influence and include bankers, lawyers, real estate professionals, consultants, and other noncompeting professionals.

  Strategic partners—All businesses have suppliers, for example, underwriters, actuaries, bankers, publishers, and many others who provide the raw ingredients that enable you to produce your product and service.

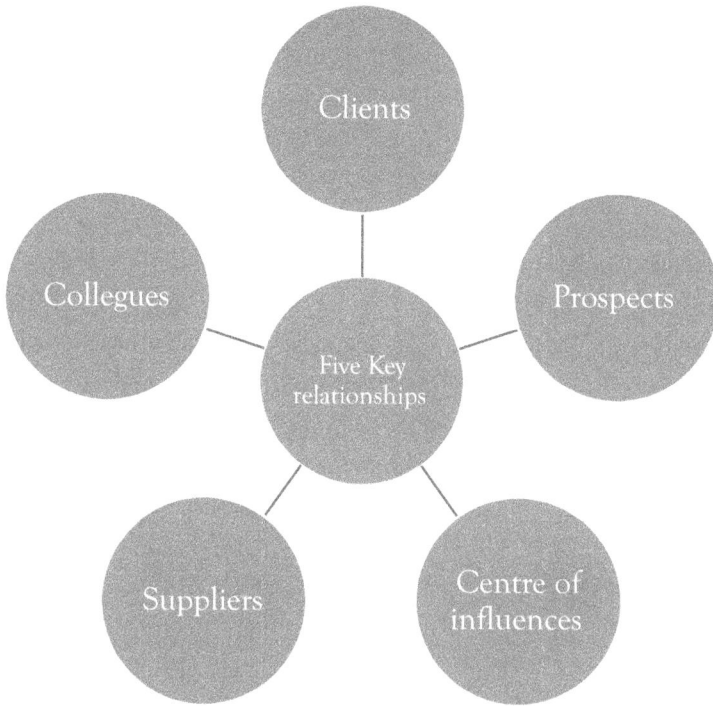

Figure 5.5 Key relationships to manage

Prospect Pipeline

Your prospect pipeline is the future success of your business. Use your new business process to create plans to proactively manage your prospective customer relationships until they hopefully become one of your top 20 percent clients. Your prospect pipeline is the result of your new business activities, when followed, should be overflowing with ideal prospective customers at various stages of the process. The focus should be on the tactics to move individuals through the multiple stages of the pipeline. The pipeline allows you to measure your conversion rate and becomes an indicator of your future business.

Account Development

Focus on the 100 percent factor, ensuring your top 20 percent clients that generate 80 per cent revenue are 100 percent clients and that you become their go-to person. On many occasions, particularly in financial services, customers may have multiple relationships firms that could easily be handled by a single professional, however, the customer is often unware of the full ranges of services the professionals firm has to offer.

Your goal is to have a 100 percent fulltime customers with a formal dates incorporated within a continuation process, that is, you have dates locked into when you are going to meet them, conduct reviews, during the year.

I was once working with a financial services firm where several professionals managed portfolios of 500 clients, generating close to half a million dollars in revenue. The majority of each professionals revenue was generated from 40 to 50 relationships. Improving services to those to 40 clients (top 20 per cent). Resulted in improved retention and increased referrals that resulted in new business.

To maximize account development, first identify your key accounts, second set up a formal dating system, and finally, follow up to build a relationship.

You will be surprised what can happen when you take a supplier out to lunch and show them your ideal client profile, educate them about your products and services, and the value you are providing. Share the type of the results that you are producing for other customers ask questions about their business and you would be surprised at how often they will be able to spot opportunities for you. Once you have identified your relationships, have a formal plan in place to manage every essential connection, keep it simple it doesn't have to be complicated.

JW is head of business development for a risk management advisory and an outstanding rain maker. Her sales pipeline is filled with referral[s] and introductions from her top 40 clients and ten centers of influences. She receives 90 per cent of her new business by reference and presentations. She meets with each of her centers of powers quarterly, averaging three meetings per month. She sees her top clients at least three times per year and regularly ask[s] and receives referrals. Her sessions are often over coffee or a sandwich; her mindset is "how can I be of assistance" to help her clients and centers of influences. This method and approach is so successful [for] her that she has little need for other types of marketing, except to follow-up on the lead through networking. Her efforts pay off for her and her firm: JW averages

30 referrals per quarter, 120 per year; she obtains appointments with 50 per cent of her leads. She finds that on average, 50 per cent of those are highly qualified and have immediate needs, and she closes between 40 and 50 per cent of those qualified leads. She maintains contact with the other points that may be qualified and have needs in the future. JW is effective [in] marketing, which generates quality and profitable business with low stress and minimal acquisition costs.

Case Study

I once was working with a wealth advisory firm that was experiencing declining revenues. There was concern about the production of their partners and advisors. The professionals complained that they did not have enough time to market. The firm was considering hiring a new person just to focus on new business development. A marketing audit revealed clients were not segmented, and professionals were trying to provide the same standard of service to everyone regardless of the revenue they produced. We categorize every client, (ABC) categories using the 80/20 rule.

The top 20 percent of client (A&B) categories represented only about 40 individual clients that needed to be actively managed, a formal plan in place to manage those 40 accounts and visit every four times a year. This dramatically improved referrals and leads as advisors remembered to ask for a reference. Advisors were spending 80 per cent of the time on the right types of activities with the right kinds of people.

Summary

- Your sales model is about the activities you need to produce top-line revenue growth objectives.
- Top professionals share common traits in terms of how they approach their business. My years as a professional salesperson and coach have led me to identify five focus skills professionals can use to succeed as rain makers.
  - Focus on markets.
  - Focus on selling system.
  - Focus on marketing.
  - Focus on continuation.
  - Focus on relationships.

CHAPTER 6

What Is Your Sales Leadership Framework?

Big shots are little shots who keep shooting.

—Christopher Morley

Rain makers are the face of your business in the battle of the marketplace. To consistently grow, there are two choices, you can hire more and more people and have them sell whatever they can or focus on quality development of your professionals and expect more from the ones you already have.

The strength of your sales leadership profoundly influences the quality and performance of a professional's sales performance. Sales leadership and sales management, however, are not one of the same. Sales management is provided by a full or part-time sales manager, whose focus is often on underperformers who lack the skill of the drive to succeed, also includes setting goals, planning, budgeting, implementing, and evaluating performance is required.

Rain makers require sale leadership, which includes properly equipping, support, strategies, and accountability. That is provided from the top by one or more people of the executive team. Figure 6.1 outlines the sales leadership framework.

The Four Elements of Your Sales Leadership Framework

First, it's equipping your professionals for success by building a cohesive team; second, providing the right support model; third, creating marketing strategies to help keep your sales pipeline filled with high quality prospective clients; and finally, building a culture of accountability.

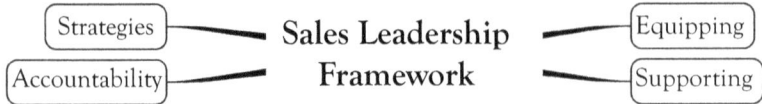

Figure 6.1 Four elements of your sales leadership

How Do You Equip Professionals for Sales Success?

This begins with defining your shared vision and mission. Your mission statement serves as a foundation for all major decisions and provides a framework to guide everyone's thinking. Your vision statement is a belief of what the future should look like for your business in the eyes of your customers, employees, and other essential stakeholders; it's designed to inspire and motivate those with a vested interest in the future of the business.

Everyone should understand their roles and responsibilities and the long-term goals of the business, with the leadership team leading by example and walking the talk. You cannot grow simply by providing better customer service; you also need to deliver first-class resources for your professionals.

Figure 6.2 shows seven ways to equip professionals:

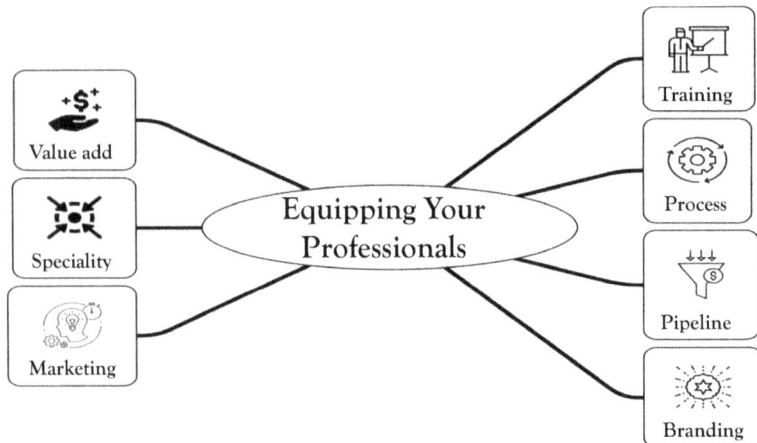

Figure 6.2 Seven ways to equip professionals for sales success

1. Training

Top performers view education and training as a means of giving their rain makers a competitive advantage. They provide education and training on technical skills (products specification, legislative) and soft skills (sales, time management, communication). Knowing is power and the key to long term growth and development of individuals and organizations.

2. Sales Process

Beginning with how to initially identify prospects and through the actual delivery and stewardship reporting once you have secured the business and covering every step along the way. A solid sales process is also a powerful training platform. The leadership team plays a crucial role in the development and ensuring that it is followed by everyone. The ideal process is continually adapted based on the experiences and collective intelligence gathered across the business.

3. Pipeline Management

The primary objective of a sales pipeline is to capture and manage information actively on prospects and existing customers. A key sales metric is the quality of your sales pipeline, ensuring it's filled with quality prospects.

4. Strong Brand

Top performers take branding seriously; they understand that it impacts their ability to write new business and retain customers and recruit professionals. Brands are not a function of an ad campaign, and the best is based on the reality of better people, service and capabilities. When a business has these capabilities, then a real competitive advantage is gained. Top sales leaders help their entire staff believe in and understand how to concisely and reasonably communicate their brand.

5. Marketing

The most fruitful sources of opportunities are those customers the business is already doing business with, the best ensure their top clients are 100 percent clients. Many professionals are leaving hundreds of thousands of dollars on the table by not fully leveraging their existing clients for new ones, cross selling and developing centers of influence.

6. Value Added Resources

Sales leaders need to provide professionals with additional value-add services. Research conducted by Reagan consulting found that financial services firms that develop in-house value-added services grew two times faster than those firms that did have in-house resources.

7. Focus

The final way to provide support is getting the right balance between being a generalist and specialist. There are two ways to specialize by industry or product or a combination. Top performers usually have built their success on, or more industry verticals and/or one or more product-focused teams. This also helps professionals focus their energy and develop specialist skills to create differentiation.

What Is the Right Type of Support?

The next step in the leadership framework is providing the right type of support that will enable your professionals to deliver results. There are three standard types of business development support models:

- Client support model
- DIY model
- Account executive model

Figure 6.3 provides an overview of three support options.

DIY Model

This works in smaller businesses, and independent professionals working as part of a larger group. The professionals receive nothing but essential support and handle most of the day-to-day service work of their accounts.

Client Support Model

Common for middle-market (mid-size) accounts. One or more specialist is teamed up with a professional to provide some technical and admin support. The professional remains significantly involved with key customers but is relieved of the burden of day-to-day servicing.

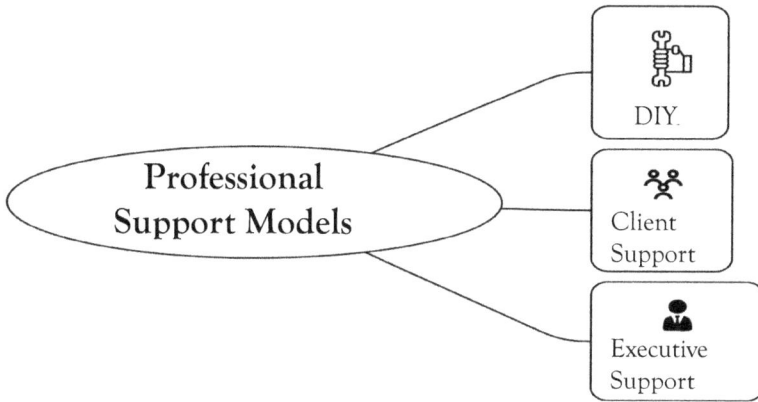

Figure 6.3 Professional support models

Account Executive Support Model

Commonly used for key accounts professionals' partner with an experienced professional (AE) with strong tech skills and relationship skills, who in conjunction with support and admin staff to handle the technical needs of clients. The difference between an experienced professional and a rain maker, experienced professionals, do not have the new business generation skills of a rain maker. AE's primary purpose is to free up rain makers to sell more new business.

The choice of support approach you use does not in itself drive growth approach; it's merely a delivery mechanism to deliver a wide range of client services.

> Example: During my selling career, I implemented and used an account executive model. I was fortunate to have skilled account executives and excellent admin staff that handled 95 per cent of the client's day-to-day needs, allowing me to focus my time and energy on filling my sales pipeline to take care of year two and year three opportunities.

What Are Your Marketing Strategies?

Formal marketing strategies maximize communication in your desired markets. There are two types of strategies, inbound (passive) to attract and gain the attention of prospective clients and outbound reaching out (proactively) to prospective clients.

Inbound strategies include:

Blogs
Advertising
Search engine optimization (SEO)
Ebooks
Podcast

Outbound marketing includes:

Direct prospecting
Telephone
Networking
Centre of influence
Existing clients

You don't have to use every strategy; however, I do recommend creating a mix of approaches based on your needs and capabilities.

Here are some guidelines:
A new professional early in their career should consider three to four outbound strategies and one to two inbound. An experienced professional: Select two to three inbound strategies and one incoming. The goal to eventually generating 75 to 80 percent of new business leads from attraction marketing methods such as referrals, introductions, and marketing events as their client base and experience grows.

How Do You Create Accountability?

A culture of accountability is driven from the top down with the leaders determining the direction they are heading and provide clear, measurable goals and expectations, and communicating this to everyone across the business. Top performers develop language and behaviors that are normal in the market, defines and continuously reinforces the culture and holds people accountable. An accountability culture guides decision making, that is intrinsic to strategy implementation.

The culture becomes a self-fulfilling prophecy. Building a culture of accountability involves sales planning, which begins with goal setting, this process is one of the activities most highly correlated to the success of the top performers, businesses that are effective at goal setting grow faster than those that are not. Effective goal setting involves much more than just establishing a number for a new business or the size of a total book of business.

It includes both activity goals and result goals. It is difficult to hold a professional accountable or even to know how best to support and equip them without an active goal setting program.

Sales leaders should work with professionals to determine their needs and areas to focus their business development efforts and determine the best strategies they will use to pursue prospective clients.

All of the previously mentioned tactics may be useful; however, the publishing of new business results is shown to be the most effective tactic, however, businesses that are struggling are more likely try to use motivation tactics than those that are prospering.

How Do You Create a Sales Culture?

Creating a sales culture is ultimately the most important thing you can do for all of your stakeholders. Top-performing businesses set high standards and hold their professionals (rain makers) accountable to those high standards. Real motivation begins with leadership. When the guidance of a professional is openly accountable to the standards it sets, personal accountability typically follows.

Accountability is less about motivation rewards and punishments than about upholding a standard that is lived out by the leadership team. Figure 6.4 shows the ten elements to building a culture of accountability.

1. Taking ownership—A study of financial services business revealed only a small percentage employing a full-time sales manager, the majority use one or more members of the executive team, or practice leader being responsible for sales manager. You don't need a full-time sales manager, the key to accountability success is having someone (or more than one) who is fully empowered with authority to take responsibility for addressing the three critical components of sales leadership.

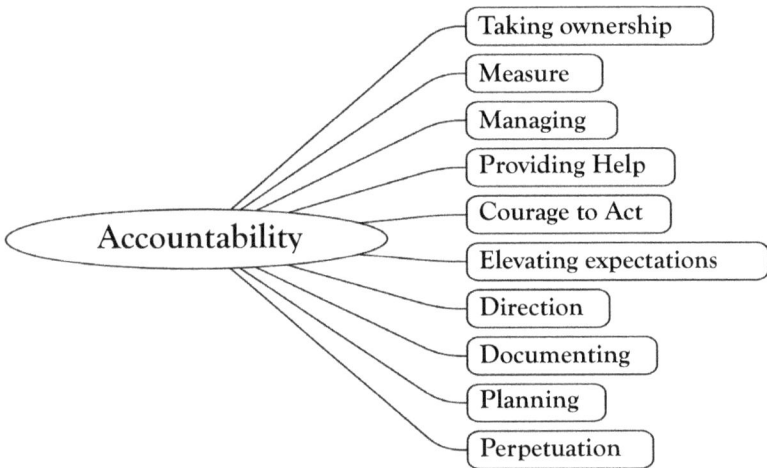

Taking ownership
Measure
Managing
Providing Help
Courage to Act
Elevating expectations
Accountability
Direction
Documenting
Planning
Perpetuation

Figure 6.4 Ten elements of accountability

2. Knowing what you want to measure—Measure results with a level of detail that allows you to understand what is happening. Also track your success and reasons for failures such as accounts won, accounts not gained, accounts lost. You can often learn more and profit from your failures.

3. Managing what you measure—Hold everyone accountable for results by managing what you measure, and if results are not being achieved, you may need to step up accountability. This can be done in several different ways, such as, meeting with professionals weekly or bi-weekly to review and discuss results and performances. Tailor the frequency and means to the person.

4. Providing help—Removing obstacles, when someone is falling short, find out why and provide the help needed. Sometimes additional education may be required, other times a change in sales

strategy and focus may be required. Some professionals may need additional support to eliminate bad habits.

5. Having courage to act—Tolerating poor performance, is frequently the achilles heel for businesses not achieving their desired results. Treating the best and worst the same is a formula for mediocrity.

6. Elevating expectations—Strive to continually raise the bar on performance. Complacency, comfort, and acceptance of poor results are a common problem with many average producing professionals. Great sales leadership continually raises the bar on the definition of acceptable behavior and outcomes.

7. Getting everyone going in the same direction—You need buy-in to create an authentic culture of accountability. Everyone providing leadership must be committed as well. Trying to create superior sales results with noncommitted leadership is extremely difficult if not impossible.

8. Delivering great client experience—Use your continuation process to defines how a client feels after they deal with you including: meetings, written and verbal communications. Your ultimate goal is to WOW your customers with every interaction and exceed their expectations.

9. Hold annual business planning process—This should be minimum a yearly planning session, with quarterly reviews and updates to hold everyone accountable to their plans. Whether you recognize it or not, you probably already have a plan of some sort. It may be located primarily in your head, in budgets, or to-do list. You should get this into a format that is understood by everyone.

10. Perpetuation—The final piece of sales leadership is perpetuation, the preserving of the legacy of your business. Perpetuation formally plans for changes in ownership, unforeseen circumstances, such as the sudden death of an owner and provide a roadmap to continually reinvigorate talent through hiring and developing. This also includes developing talent.

Do you have clear plans and strategies?

The key to consistent and robust growth, but also effective top performers, is to pay careful attention to what works and does not work, and often have a significant advantage over their peers. Long gone are the days of merely providing a professional with an office and list and expect them to sell something.

Many of today's top-performing businesses build sophisticated training and mentoring programs that cover a wide range of technical and sales skills tailored to the needs of the individual. This is one advantage of specialization is that it can allow for faster and more meaningful professional development. Mentoring programs can materially enhance success rates—experience professionals take responsibility for growth and success of younger producers.

As a sales leader, you will need to help determine the plans, process, and timing for professional recruitment; this can be internal or external and involve the whole management team in the active participation recruitment. However, it's the sales leader's need to be the one within the business, who is continually thinking about, developing strategy, and driving the recruiting activities.

For example, many financial services firms hiring professionals under the age of 30 prefer to hire from outside the industry, while firms hiring professionals over 30 predominantly pursue these candidates from inside the industry, usually from a competitor. Hiring new professionals is different than hiring more experienced ones. While new professionals are relatively inexpensive, they will require a more significant investment in training, mentoring, and development. As a sales leader, you should look both inside and outside for potential talent at your culture, resources, and goals before deciding which hiring direction to pursue.

Case Study

I was a sales leader for a multinational company and always on the lookout for promising talent who could help me and the organization fulfill its growth objectives. PT joined our business as a temporary working in the mail room. I had an urgent need to fill a sales position and decided to advertise internally. PT expressed interest and I was surprised to discover during my interview at how qualified he was. I hired PT on a six-month probation, however, I made him permanent after just six weeks. I learned a valuable lesson that sometime your best talent can right under your nose.

Summary

- The strength of sales leadership profoundly influences the quality and performance of professional's sales performance.
- There are three elements: first, it's equipping your professionals for success by building a cohesive team, providing the right support; second, creating formal inbound and outbound marketing strategies to keep sales pipeline filled with high quality prospective clients; and finally, building a culture of accountability.

CHAPTER 7

What Is Your Sales Direction Framework?

A salesman, like the storage battery in your car, is constantly discharging energy unless he is recharged at frequent intervals, he soon runs dry. This is one of the greatest responsibilities of sales leadership.

—Richard Grant

Your sales direction is how you execute your sales plans to achieve your goals, retention and revenue, and grow your business.

The Five Essential Areas of Your Sales Direction Framework

There are five key areas in your sales direction framework: first, there is your annual sales plans, the tactics to acquire and retain customers; second, developmental coaching to manage of your sales pipeline to track prospective customers through your process; third, creating a coaching culture to hold everyone accountable; fourth, coaching to provide sales support and professional development; and finally, providing feedback to track results and providing help if required. Figure 7.1 provides an overview of the sales management framework.

What Are Annual Sales Plans?

Every professional responsible for business development requires an individual annual sales plan. This forms the basis for their key performance indicators (KPI's) for accountability. A professionals sales plane should contain:

New business
Retention
Capabilities

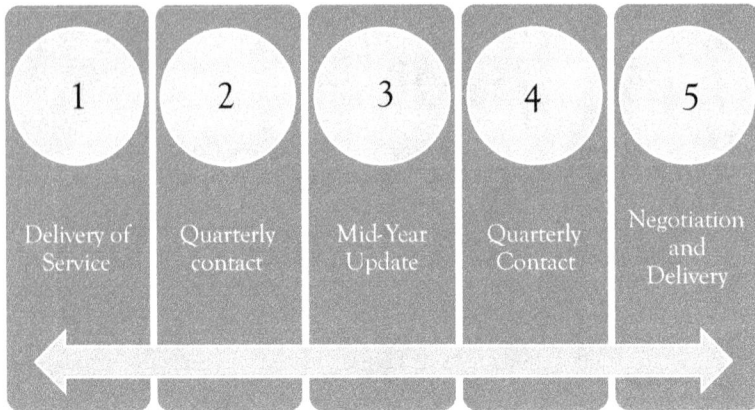

Figure 7.1 Sales management framework

New Business

The number of new customers to be acquired over the next year, in total numbers and overall growth from the prior year to expand the client base.

Retention

This is more than just retaining a client number, it also includes the revenue associate with a customer. Customer revenue can be affected by price changes, market conditions, and competitors stealing your accounts. This means you can have excellent client retention (number of clients) and still go backwards in terms of revenue. Top professionals maximize customer retention by first ensuring all of their desirable clients are 100 percent full-time.

Capabilities

The final part of the annual sales plans is assessing your behaviors and capability requirements to achieve the desired results. These should be included in your annual plan and strategies to acquire them. Skills and capabilities improvements include time management, prospecting, relationship management. Finally and most importantly, all the sales plans should align with the overall business growth plans.

What Is Developmental Coaching?

Developmental coaching is the single most important thing you can do as a sales leader to increase productivity and to meet and exceed your business plans. It's an incremental process of helping people get to the next level, by ensuring their improvement in business performance and relationships. This is something as a leader you can control, when done well you will develop individual breakthrough relationships with your professionals and ultimately your clients, this is something competitors cannot easily duplicate. Coaching can become your business's secret weapon.

Why Does It Work?

Everyone has blind spots that are too close to perceive completely and clearly, coaching can help professionals turn these into perspective and without coaching, people will not change and develop fast enough to meet the demands of your business. Developing people is much cheaper than hiring and firing, and developing people is a much more effective way to professionally reach their full potential. Generally, I have found most professionals that I have worked with in organizations are hungry for coaching and feedback. I believe everyone needs and deserves feedback and developmental coaching is the ideal method.

Money is often left on the table when there is no coaching. This money in the form of energy, ideas, skill, talent, as well as hard cash. Not being able to develop 100 percent full-time accounts and retain key accounts are two examples of this. Developmental coaching is about how to change by doing things differently.

For the sales leader, developmental coaching is an ideal way to get a bird's eye view of what's happening with prospective customers and key accounts, and it also helps to keep your skills sharp, which can happen when someone moves into management. Coaching makes each day a new beginning in which the leader and their people continually get better and you will quickly pick up and correct gaps in your own sales process.

There are three reasons why developmental coaching works. First, it teaches the professionals the process of removing obstacles themselves over time. This reduces the dependency on the sales leader or coach. Second, it makes the other parts of the job of a sales leader more enjoyable.

Finally, it makes everyone including the sales leader a better salesperson by encouraging a vision of excellence fostering a passion to achieve excellence continually and incrementally.

Five reasons why leaders don't coach

1. Not enough time—Sales leaders often have multiple management responsibilities and sales management is a part of it; some have their own clients and portfolios to manage.
2. No role models—They have never been coached themselves during their career, and there is no one they can model or follow.
3. Don't know how—It means they don't know what they don't know, gap in knowledge. Of course, if a leader never experiences coaching during their career, it's difficult to appreciate the benefits.
4. No incentive—There is no accountability for the leader to coach or it's loosely defined in their role and responsibilities.
5. Managers are knighted—It's not unusual for the top salesperson to be promoted into management often with little or no training.

How Do You Create a Coaching Culture?

To make the leap from leader to coach does not require a change to the structure of your business and as a leader you are in a unique position to be the catalyst for change. Figure 7.2 outlines building a coaching culture. The first step is understanding what's in your control; second, understand the four zones; third, conduct regular sales meetings; and finally, providing the right type of feedback.

Understanding what's in your control

We have discussed that many businesses don't have full-time sales managers and often the role of sales leadership is shared among one or more members of the leadership team. The person responsible needs to have the authority and influence in the business, evaluate and/or contribute to the compensation system to support coaching and be committed to helping their professionals reach the next level.

Everyone should know and understand what a great future customer looks like for them and the business. This includes the traits of your best clients what they look like, where they are located, problems, concerns, and challenges they face.

It's OK and often advisable to have one or more marketing niches and industries you are serving, develop an ideal buyer profile for each of these to be clear on what a great client looks like. It should be clearly articulated what a top client looks like, smells like, and sounds like; the best place to begin is by looking at the characteristics and traits of your very best clients.

Follow the 80:20 rule to review your top 20 percent customers. List down the traits that make them a great client, for example, they pay on time, have problems and needs that are within your capabilities, they are within your geographic location, the owners or leaders are willing to form a partnership with you, and you learned from them, easy to work with, and a continual learning experience.

After you have identified and agreed on what a great future customer looks like, focus your marketing efforts on building an overflowing sales pipeline. Your sales process becomes the stages in your sales pipeline, and your job is monitoring the flow of people through the process and what stage they are at and the actions required to move a prospective client or a client from one stage to the next.

I was once involved in a sale that took over five years to close. Since we had robust and thorough process, it was easy to work out what actions needed to take place to keep things on track. During this time, there were several personal changes on the buyers side and I did not become involve until a year or two into the process, when I acquired it from my predecessor.

Hold Regular Sales Meetings

Sales meetings held monthly, bi-weekly, or weekly helps everyone to stay on track. Sales meetings should be focused on the sales pipeline and what needs to be done to convert prospects and manage key relationships. The purpose is to define the business development opportunity requiring immediate priority action and to address specifically to have detailed discussions on critical strategies, action that needs to be taken, by whom and when.

Three Questions leaders should ask during sales meetings:

Are we on track on our individual and group sales plans?
Are our behaviors and strategies developing the right behaviors and habits?
Have you clearly identifying what's in the pipeline and the actions needed to move prospective clients to the next stage and eventually convert them into clients?

The Sales Meeting Format

Designate a specific day of the week, time, and duration for the business development meeting—weekly, fortnightly, or monthly.

- Each professional defines and maintains a weekly updated list of their top 10 highest priority business development opportunities based upon the designated qualification priority attributes as well as all the essential account background and progress data essential in the methodical closing of each account.
- All the account data and information maintained and updated on a centrally accessible sales information system and will be a primary responsibility of each professional.
- Each professional will submit all the account update information on each of their top 10 accounts along with an updated prioritization ranking prior to the scheduled weekly meeting. They will also include the complete account profile of their top two accounts for detailed account strategy discussions during the meeting.
- Take detailed notes regarding all the key follow-up priorities so as to insure 100 percent follow through. If for any reason, anyone feels uncertain of complying with any designated target dates, this is the time to speak out.

- When someone senses their designated target date may not be achieved, they are to contact the appropriate Point of Contact as early as possible in an effort to mobilize a contingency strategy if necessary.
- These meetings do not have to be long, but they do need to be regular and preferably scheduled at the same time. For new professionals, these meeting should be held weekly; for experience professionals, they can be bi-weekly and no more than monthly. They can be 15, 20, 30 minutes long, but put together, a thorough agenda that addresses the key issues.

Holding regular sales meetings will ensure that nothing slips through the cracks. Key accounts don't decide to leave overnight. Also, major accounts are not won overnight, but through a series of steps. Discussions during regular sales meeting will ensure that nothing is left to chance.

What Is The Right Zone?

There will be occasions when a professional can be in the wrong zone (space) for coaching help. Understanding the different zones a professional operates in can help you to become an effective coach and leader. Figure 7.2 outlines the four zones.

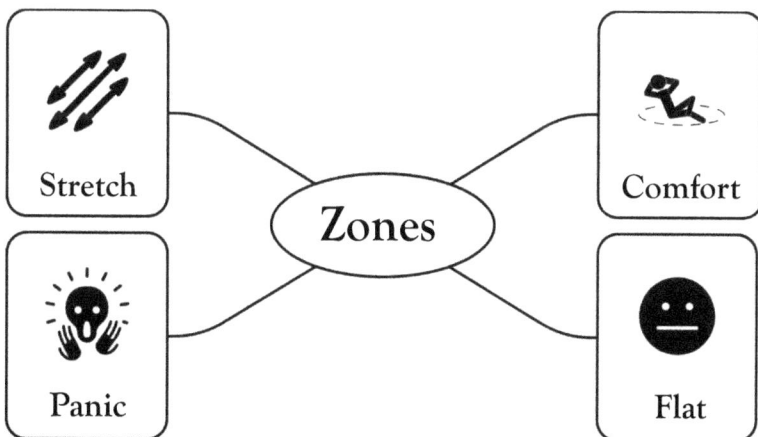

Figure 7.2 The four zones

Zone 1:

Flat zone—Professionals in this zone are not interested in improving, they have stopped learning and improving, they are disengaged. You can find professionals who are waiting to retire or have retired mentally some time ago and just bidding their time.

Zone 2:

Comfort zone—Professionals in this area want to be effective. In many cases, they may have enjoyed success and just want to do the things that have worked for them in past. While they appear to be successful, they can often have blinders and fail to see change.

Zone 3:

Panic zone—Professionals here are reactive. They cannot learn well and feel out of control and under pressure. Burnout happens in this zone as selling is no longer fun; some of people may have previously been in the comfort zone for too long.

Zone 4:

Stretch zone—The best place to be. Professionals in this zone are at their best, committed to learning. A good coach can be a catalyst for change. Incremental planned development one step at a time is the ideal way to develop people in this zone. People do move back and forth between the zones, but stabilize in one place for at least a period of time.

Learn to understand and recognize your own zone as well as those of your team. Newer professionals may feel they are in a constant panic zone as they seek to learn and grow as fast as possible. Veterans in the comfort zone quickly move move to the dead or panic zone if left unchecked.

What is Feedback?

Feedback is crucial in developing professionals into rain makers and sustaining performance over the long term. There are two types of feedback:

evaluative and developing an understanding of their differences. How and when to use each type will have a big impact on your coaching success.

Evaluative Feedback

This is often the type of feedback most people are used to, provided during performance reviews on a quarterly or annually, it is more one way and focuses on the individual. This is necessary to present a picture of what has happened in the past. This type of feedback is often formalized and paperwork-driven, such as performance of pay reviews.

Developmental Feedback

Is forward looking aimed at improving future performance. It answers the questions "What can we do better to meet or exceed the objective?" These types of questions should asked regularly. Developmental feedback empowers because it helps everyone to identify obstacles and moves them into the stretch zone. Developmental feedback and coaching helps make evaluative feedback more enjoyable.

Case Study

A financial services firm struggling with retention, several key accounts were lost due to the poor service. Clients were not categorized, a category "C" client was receiving "A" class service as staff were unable to prioritize and were able to identify a key client until it's too late. The business also didn't have a continuation process to monitor client activity, which meant the account professionals and leadership were constantly reactive putting out fires to save accounts.

With everyone focused on trying to save business, growth stalled as nobody was focusing on new business. The business was eventually sold at a low price to try to salvage something. The previous leadership wound up working as account managers for the new owner and entered the dead zone. They were eventually moved on from the business.

Summary

- There five key areas in your sales direction framework, pipeline management, and accountability.
- Everyone should know and understand what a great future client looks likes. Every professional with a responsibility for business development requires an individual annual sales plan.
- Recruitment should be an ongoing process; the worst mistake is being reactive instead of proactive.
- Developmental coaching works, it teaches the professionals the process of removing obstacles themselves over time this reduces the dependency on the sales leader/coach.
- Coaching makes the other parts of the job of a sales leader more enjoyable. Finally, it makes everyone including the sales leader a better salesperson by encouraging a vision of excellence, fostering a passion to achieve excellence continually and incrementally.

CHAPTER 8

What's Your Marketing Framework?

Marketing is everything.

—Regis McKenna

The fundamentals of marketing and selling have not changed, however, modern marketing has become slicker and more expensive with more choices. Today's buyers have more choice and are more sophisticated, harder to impress, less satisfied, and less loyal. Top professionals understand they compete for relationships, and customers have an opportunity to learn about their offerings in many ways that has nothing to sales pitches. In today's marketing, you are the product and your success hinges on your relationships, the quality of your work, and it ends and begins with results.

For decades, marketers have relied on the Four Ps of marketing, product, place, promotion, and price to sell their products. Today the Four Ps are no longer enough in today's busy and crowed market—place and especially in selling professional services. Your marketing mix needs to be extended to include five marketing principals to provide a single framework and lay the foundation for implementing marketing plans, developing and training your people.

The Five Essential Areas of Your Marketing Framework

There are five key areas in your marketing framework: first; there is your position, second; is planning your message, third; packaging of your ideas and expertise, fourth; promotion and finally, personel selling. Figure 8.1 provides an overview of these five principals.

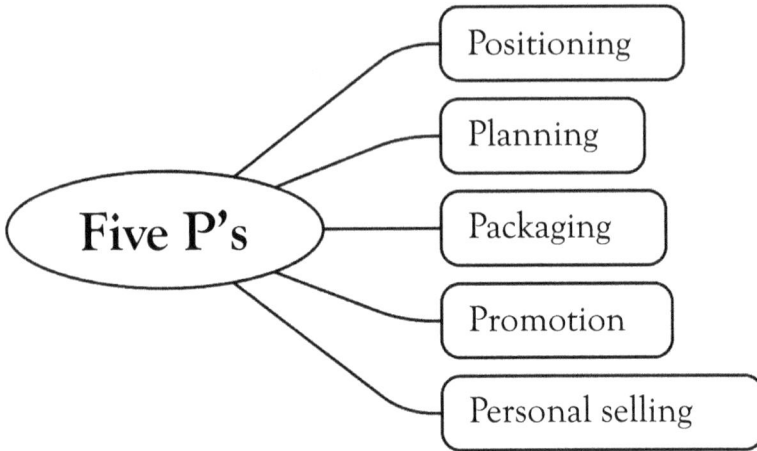

Figure 8.1 Five marketing principal

Principal 1: Positioning

This is an organized process for finding the entry point in the mind of your customers. It involves thinking about your market and what's important to the people in it; this is also how you want to be known within your desired markets and niches, where you want to focus and how you want to be seen. There are six positioning questions that when combined help you achieve a strong position in your target markets. The six positioning questions are:

1. How do we position our business with targets of opportunities?
   Answer this question by describing the nature of your business, state clearly your mission and purpose for being in business.
2. How do we position our business against competitors?
   State how you are different and how you are better from known competitors. List the factors that make your business different.
3. How do we position our professionals with targets of opportunities?
   Communicate your professional's education, training, what they do for customers and why they are truly valuable to the targets.
4. How do we position our alliance partners with targets of opportunities?

Alliance partners are cooperative relationships you have with others and add complementary skills and resources to your capabilities.

5. How do we position our solutions with targets of opportunities? Outline your competitive fees, experience, and innovated solutions

6. How do we position our solutions against the competition? communicate about your business that makes your solution different, dig deep to find areas that are perceived by the customer as being only or more readily available from you than from others offering your solution.

Principal 2: Planning

The purpose of a marketing plan is to articulate how your will attract and retain profitable customers to your business. It provides a roadmap and destination to achieve your growth objectives. Here are five questions to consider when developing your marketing plan:

Why are our services and products needed?
Why should customers buy from us?
What benefits do we provide?
What is our competitive situation?
Who cares whether we are in business?

Understand your plan may not follow at straight path to your destination, expect twist and turn. Focus on doing a few things exceptionally well, when developing your plans, carefully choose your goals for example:

- Number of customers
- Improving marketing visibility
- New relationships to forge
- Revenue, profits, and growth
- New products and services you would like to develop and introduce
- Expanding scope of current products and services to existing customers

Principal 3: Packaging

Packaging is how you present your knowledge and expertise to your marketplace. You should package your business and your professionals, verbally and in writing. Verbal packaging is the language your professionals use to describe what they do, sometimes described as a value proposition or elevator speech when someone is asked, "What do you do?" Written packaging includes, success stories, customer list; your products, services, brochures, website, business card.

All of this comes together in your proposals, meetings, and referral sources. Packaging forms a key part of your plans that enables you to position and stand out from others.

Principal 4: Promotion

Is how you communicate to your desired markets to gain visibility, attention, and credibility with existing and prospective customers to ensure your brand, products, services messages are reaching your intended audience to ensure your business is not one of the world's best kept secrets.

Promotion falls into two categories: direct (Reach out) and indirect (attraction), and an effective promotional plan combines these two.

Attraction promotion includes advertising, social media, public relations, trade shows, brochures, web, and publications. For example, some rain makers attract their business by joining clubs that attract their ideal buyers, they get to know these members through networking and serving on committees developing a relationship of trust. When a potential buyer is facing an issue or challenge, he will reach out to his fellow club to discuss. This type of rain making whilst effective, can take time to build.

Direct promotion is where you physically reach out to your target market instead of waiting for the phone to ring. Too many businesses wait for the phone ring because they do not have an effective pro-active marketing program. Tactics include direct mail, e-mail, telephone, networking, referrals, and centers of influence. Top rain makers are effective in both types of promotional approaches.

You must follow up because, not everyone will respond in fact, the majority of who you contact will not respond. The good news is that you only need a small percentage, a basic marketing rule is that you must

- ❶ Prospect and Qualify
- ❷ Pre approach
- ❸ Approach

Personal Selling ——— ❹ Presentation

- ❺ Objections
- ❻ Closing
- ❼ Follow

Figure 8.2 Sales process

pursue many to win a few. The probability of turning any single person or lead into a new client is probably small, however, by pursuing many you stack the odds in your favor as the probability of any specific target becoming a client is much more. As you will learn, there are things you can do to decrease the number of prospects you have to pursue to win.

Principal 5: Personal Selling

Rain makers are masters in the art of personal selling, the most cost-effective way to establishing and maintaining customer relationships. There are two approaches to selling sales oriented and customer centric, which consist of professionalism, negotiation, and relationship marketing. The customer centric approach trains professionals in customer problem solving. They learn how to listen and question in order to identify customer needs and come up with solutions. The key is using an effective sales process. Figure 8.2 is an example of a sales process

Step 1 Prospecting and qualifying

> The first step is to identify your ideal prospects, methods include:
> Referrals from existing clients
> Networking by joining organizations where prospective clients belong
> Developing centers of influence
> Engaging in speaking and writing

Step 2 Pre approach

Researching prospects hot button needs, buying criteria and decision makers. Plan contact method such a email, mail and/or phone to make initial contact.

>   Direct mail
>   Cold calling
>   Pre approach

Rain makers find ways to turn cold calls into warm opportunities. Researching establish objectives, identify the decision maker, gathering information, developing an account strategy.

Step 3 Approach

What to say after "hello" once you land a first meeting with a prospective client?

The opening must include some key questions to help build rapport.

Step 4 Presentation

There are three approaches to conducting an effective presentation, the oldest is the canned approach, where you memorize a sales talk covering the main points. The formulated approach—the buyer's needs, and attitudes are identified early during the discussion, the salesperson then shows how the product or service will satisfy their needs. This not a canned presentation but follows a general plan. Customer centered approach begins with a search of a client's real needs by encouraging the client to do most of the talking. This calls for good listening and problem-solving skills.

Top rain makers follow the centered approach. When structuring your sales-presentation a good formula to use is the AIDA, gaining attention, holding interest, arousing desire, and obtaining action. This is where you tell your product or service story to the buyer, using the benefits (advantages) and features (the characteristics) a common mistake is dwelling on product features instead of the clients' benefits (a market orientation).

Step 5 Handling Objections

Buyers will pose objections during the presentation or when asked for the order, this resistance can psychological or logical. Psychological includes reluctance to giving up something, fear of change, and apathy. Logical resistance includes, price, timing, existing contractual arrangements, or company characteristics. The best way to handle objections is by preparing and anticipating them in advance.

Step 6 Closing

This is often an area many professionals struggle with. Sometimes they lack confidence or feel uncomfortable about asking for the sale, or simply do recognize the right psychological moments that indicate the buyer is ready. The sales can be closed by summarizing the conversation in a proposal or asking the client to sign an agreement.

Step 7 Follow up

Following up and continued maintenance are necessary to ensure client retention and obtaining referrals. The professional should develop an account plan and calendar that aligns with the steps of your sales process. This should be customized for each client.

What skills do your professionals require?

Critical skills are those things you must do that determine you success or failure. If you do them well, you acheive success and if you do them poorly, or do some well, your overall results will still be poor.

Table 8.1 shows the 10 critical skills of top rain makers:

Table 8.1 Critical rain making skills

1. Selling system—Follow a common process
2. Sales Pipeline—Understand what future client looks like
3. Time focus—80 percent of time spent on sales activities
4. Relationship management—Active plans in place
5. Referrals—75 percent of new business generated from referrals
6. Account development—System to develop 100 percent clients
7. Retention strategies—Plans to retain all desirable clients
8. Centre of influences—Non client referral sources
9. Target account size—Minimum size for new accounts
10. Specialist focus—Identified 1 to 3 niche markets

1. Selling System

A companywide selling system that is followed by everyone for acquiring new business. This selling system forms part of your sales pipeline also becomes a critical part of how you show prospective customers how you will work with them.

2. Sales Pipeline

There should be absolute clarity on what an ideal future customer looks like, their traits, characteristics, and location. You want your rain makers to maintain overflowing sales pipeline that matches your sales process so that you can manage each stage of the process.

3. Time Focus

The ability to spend the acquired amount of time on sales related activities that should be around 80 percent related to sales related activities, consisting of results, relationships, referrals, and working with centers of influence to obtain introductions.

4. Relationship Management

To ensure you have 100 percent full-time customers, your continuation program needs to be implemented for every customer in your top 20 percent category. This includes dates locked in for meeting with your buyer and a service calendar established.

5. Referrals

This forms part of year unique competitive advantage of referrals. Ultimately, the majority of your new business (75–80 percent) generated from referrals from your best customers. To develop referral relationships by asking on a regular basis through your sales process to ensure a steady flow of prospective customers in your pipeline.

6. Account Development

A system in place to develop key customer accounts into full-time 100 percent customers.

7. Retention Strategies

Retain 100 percent of all desirable customers and accounts by building exit rings.

8. Center of Influences

Establish non client referral relationships to provide referrals and introduction's to your ideal clients.

9. Target Account Size

Establishing a minimum account size for prospective new customers.

10. Specialist Focus

Niche and specialty markets to become an expert in and develop leads and appointments with prospective customers.

Principal 6:

What Is Performance?

Performance is about taking care of your five key relationships clients, prospects, centers of influence (COI), team members, and strategic partners to leverage these relationships make marketing your products and services easier. Performance is high touch you have a service-oriented approach to marketing and selling your customer relationship needs are paramount. Figure 8.3 illustrates five areas of performance.

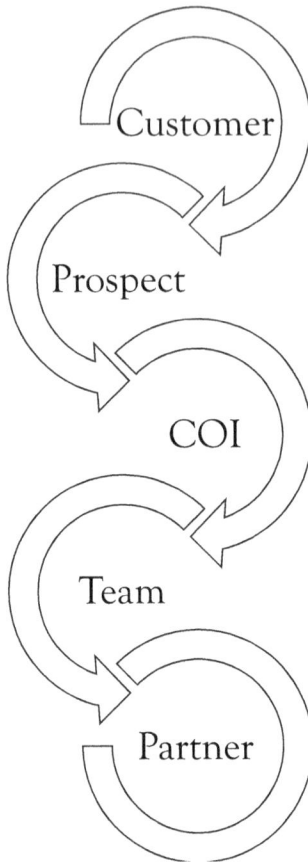

Figure 8.3 Five areas of performance

What Is Customer Performance?

Customer performance is not something you do, it's something you are, it's about energy commitment, caring and excellence. The seven performance qualities of top rain makers are:

1. Honesty—Not making exaggerated claims about your products, services, or capabilities.
2. Discipline—Being consistent, returning phone calls, following up, and providing accurate information.
3. Getting along with people—Following the 95/5 rule

4. Going the extra mile—Focusing on the things that matter for customers and delivers high value whilst providing a great ROI for everyone.

5. Loving what you do—You enjoy your and responsibility of helping others.

6. Leadership—Strive to be the leader in your chosen market niche(s).

7. Competitive spirit—Turn performance into a game where you are constantly raising the bar on the level of performance.

Prospect Performance

Prospect performance begins once you identify, enter prospect, and track them in your pipeline as they move through your marketing cycle. You want your sales pipeline to be filled with your ideal clients, those prospects with the characteristics and traits of your very best customers.

Centre of Influence Performance (COI)

Centre of influence performance is about continually educating nonclient referral sources on ways they can help you. Keep them up to date and be clear on your needs and requirements so they better help you in terms of introductions and leads to fill your sales pipeline. COI's vouch for your statements to prospects on whom you need or want to make a favorable impression, enabling you to leverage your time and resources.

Team Performance

Your team performance is ensuring everyone is working together to achieve 100 percent retention of all desirable customers. Retention, continuation, and relationship systems are in place to retain those clients. The team is 100 percent focused on serving the customer to acquire 100 percent of their business.

Strategic Partners Performance

Strategic partner performance in ensuring you are leveraging your relationships to your competitive advantage. Create a win-win partnership by always asking questions, being creative, curious, and passionate about you world. Your strategic partnerships help you multiply your capabilities and extending your reach makes it easier to develop and maintain 100 percent full-time customers.

Case Study

I used to run a direct marketing business in the insurance sector. Using targeted mailing to offer personal insurance to affinity groups, the average response was around 2 percent. A mailing sent to 20,000 individuals resulted in 400 new policies. The average premium for the first year was $75, we also had a good nurturing system that delivered predictable results, over a period of three-to-five years a customer paying $75 in year one, if they were nurtured through cross selling and upselling, many of these client were paying $500 per year by the end of year five. This same principle applies for all of your desired customer accounts.

Summary

- Your marketing framework is an offensive strategy (system) for attracting and acquiring new accounts.
- It's how you develop new business, leverage it for growth, eventually turn it into them from part time to full time accounts over the next two three, or four year period.
- It's also your defensive strategy—to prevent a competitor from attacking your accounts by having a very clearly defined system pro-actively partnering with your customer to educate them on your offerings and value.
- The fundamentals of marketing and selling have not changed, however, modern marketing has become slicker and more expensive with more choices.

- Today's buyers have more choice and are more sophisticated, harder to impress, less satisfied, and less loyal. Top professionals today understand they compete for relationships, and customers can learn about their offerings in many ways that has nothing to sales pitches. In today's marketing, you are the product and your success hinges on your relationships, the quality of your work and it ends and begins with results.
- The Four P's of marketing are no longer enough. Your marketing mix needs to be extended to include six marketing principals: positioning, planning, packaging, promotion, personal selling, performance.

PART III

Building Your Rain making Team

CHAPTER 9

Developing and Implementing Sales Plans

If you don't know where you are going, any road will get you there.
—Lewis Carroll

What is a Strategic Sales Plan?

A strategic sales plan is your roadmap, in fact there is a good change that you already have a sales plan that could be formal or informal in your mind, on a to-do list, or your budgets and targets. Regardless of the type of plan, the goal is still the same, to convert your ideas and intentions into actions. Sales plans help turn professionals into rain makers and drive new business growth.

Planning can be divided into two parts: strategic, focusing on the future direction of the business and its environment, and tactical, focusing on the short-term time frame of one year.

You need both strategic and tactical plans; the former leads to the latter, however, the two cannot be done at the same time. A major cause of stagnant growth is due to a business inability to effectively implement their tactical plans. I have seen business do an OK job developing a strategic side but are unable to formulate and execute the right tactics. Figure 9.1 outlines the flow from strategy to tactical.

The process of developing a strategy is beyond the scope of this book, additional resources are provided in the appendix. This chapter is about creating tactics that will provide a roadmap to turn your professionals into top rain makers. It starts with management establishing the (What)

Figure 9.1 Strategy versus Tactics

future direction and the sales leader creating the (how) to produce the required short-term results.

Strategic sales plan contains the following six elements:

Determining focus
Identifying critical issues
Selecting what will be measured
Deciding on targets
Creating action plans
Reviewing and monitoring plans

You can include more factors in your strategic sales plan, but the afore-mentioned elements have proven to be useful for many businesses.

How do you determine your focus?

Your focus are the key results areas (KRA), the categories of results that are essential to effective performance and consider all stakeholders, shareholders, employees, customers, and so on. Your focus provides the continuity in plans from year to year. Begin by identifying the five-to-eight major areas where you must achieve meaningful results during the coming year. Identify both financial and nonfinancial areas, choose areas that directly or indirectly support the overall strategic plan.

It's important to choose the vital few areas where your priority areas should be directed in instead of trying to cover everything. Limit each of your KRA's to two or three words that contain factors that could be made measurable and should be specific enough to identify the kind of results needed and flexibility to cover more than one specific result.

Examples of focus KRA's:

Revenue/sales
Return/profit
Growth percentage
New market development
New customers
Customer retention

How do identify critical issues?

Critical issues are the specific areas that will have significant impact on your business during the coming year. They provide a link between your strategy and tactics and provide the basis for selecting the vital few four to eight key result areas that will impact your results.

Here are the four steps to analyze your critical issues:

1. Indentify
2. Prioritize
3. Analyze
4. Summarize

Identify

Review your KRAs, identify any potential issues, problems, and challenges and ask the following questions:

(a) What are the most critical issues we are facing in the coming year?
(b) What impact will each of these have on our performance?
(c) What issues are likely to make the greatest contribution to long-term success?

(d) What resource limitations or opportunities need to be addressed?

(e) What changes have taken place or likely to take place during the coming year that will significantly affect my performance?

Prioritize

(a) Agree on the four to eight most important issues.

Analyze issues

(a) What is the issue?

(b) What data or information is available to either validate or invalidate this issue?

(c) What evidence is there to justify putting the time and effort into resolving this?

Summarize issues

(a) What conclusions can be drawn from this analysis that will provide direction for specific action?

(b) What are the alternative ways of acting on your conclusion?

(c) How do you select what to measure?

How Do You Select What to Measure?

Key performance indicators describe what is to be measured, they are the factors within your KRAs that you wish to and are worthwhile to set specific objectives. The primary purpose of KPIs is to identify the kind of measurable output desired in each of your KRAs. They describe what will be measured, not how much or by when, (That is covered in objetives) they provide the relevant information for tracking desired results. The primary purpose of KPIs is to establish the right objectives at the right time.

There are three guidelines to developing your KRIs:

1. They should be measurable select from any of the following:
   Numbers
   Percentages

Service factors

Soft or indirect indicators

2. They should identify what will be measured—not the how and what.

3. They should represent factors that can be tracked on an ongoing basis

How do you choose your targets?

Your targets are the objectives and standards you wish to be accomplished in the next 12 months. These should be limited to your most important accomplishments from the conclusions reached during your critical issues' analysis.

Guidelines:

Four to seven objectives with written action plans is a good number to aim for.

Here are five guidelines when choosing your objectives:

(a) Objectives should start with the word "to" be followed by an action verb.
(b) Specify a singular measurable result. Specify a target date or time span. Specify maximum cost.
(c) Be as specific and quantitative as possible.
(d) Specify only the what and when, and not the how and why.
(e) Should be realistic and attainable—but still a stretch.

Reaching your targets

Objectives are action commitments you make, and when they are fortified by action, they lead to a measurable result and another term for measurable result is goal. The nature, scope, and potential of your development as a rain maker will depend on the objectives you establish.

First distinguish between your required and desired objectves.

Required objectives must be accomplished for the business to survive. Examples of objectives in this category include:

Acquisition of new customers on a regular basis during the year.
Retention, holding on to 100 percent of your desired customers.
Customer profitability purchased products and services that generate good profit margins.

Desired objectives.
Differ from required objectives in that they may be something that you strongly want, but they are not required for the survival of the business. Examples include:

Moving into new markets.
Creating new services to attract higher fees.
Replacing lost revenue of smaller customers.

When setting objectives should only act on those desired objectives that you feel really strong about and that are very important for the business. You should periodically review your objectives as shown in Figure 9.2.

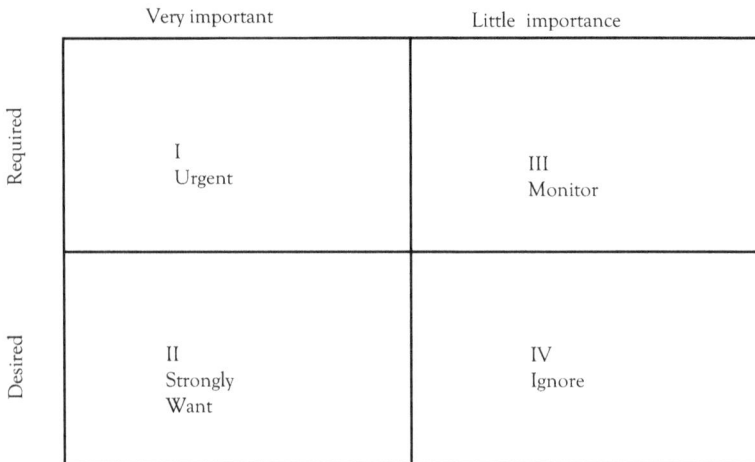

	Very important	Little importance
Required	I Urgent	III Monitor
Desired	II Strongly Want	IV Ignore

Figure 9.2 Goal setting diagram

Category 1—Very important and required. These are urgent things that need to done in order to survive for example, getting new customers or removing unprofitable business.

Category 2—Very important and desired. Things you may strongly want but are not critical to the success of the business, for example, expanding into a niche market.

Category 3—Little importance but required. These should be monitored and reclassified if necessary, for example the slow payment of certain accounts.

Category 4—Little importance and desired. Ignore these

Your priority is to handle everything in category one and then focus on category two, monitor category three to decide if it needs to be shifted to category one or two. Finally, ignore category four. Following the previous diagram will help ensure you are focusing on the right activities at the right time.

In developing the growth of your business, you could establish many classes of objectives. Here are seven most frequently used classifications:

1. Industry objectives—Goals to penetrate niche markets develop relationships and specialization.
2. Personal objectives—Developing capabilities and skills to survive and generate sales.
3. Service objectives—Creating and leveraging services that provide a competitive advantage.
4. Strategic objectives – Focus on tomorrow, future direction of the business.
5. Operational objectives—Improving productivity.
6. Product objectives—Having access competitive products to meet the needs of clients and prospective clients.
7. Relationship objectives—Maintaining breakthrough relationships with clients, prospects, referral sources, and strategic partners.

Figure 9.3 shows a list of objectives you may wish to consider.

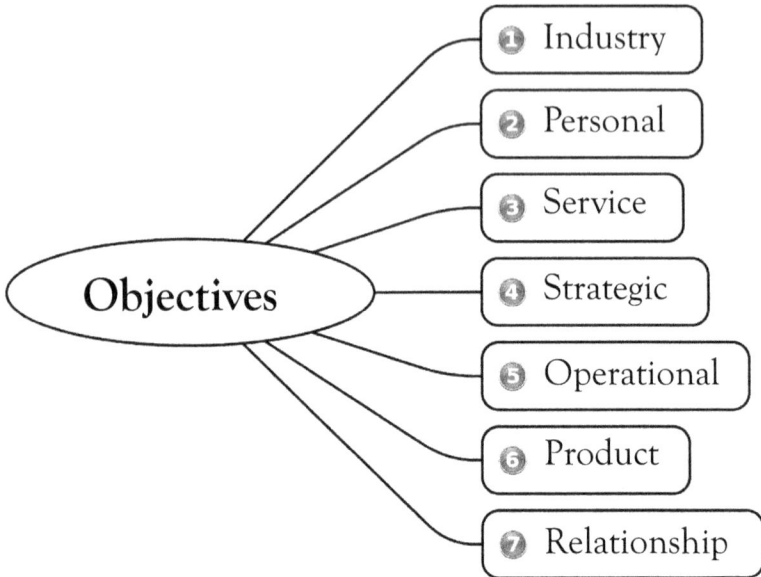

Figure 9.3 Objective rating sheet (Map graphic)

Step 2: Scan the previous list and choose no more than three to five objectives.

When selecting the objectives, more is not better.

Instead, focus on moving a few things a mile instead moving several things an inch. Choosing objectives may seem easy, however, the task should be not taken lightly. The objectives you choose will literally define the future of your business. Define the specific objectives that you want your professionals to achieve. For example:

(a) Time spent with current clients, prospects.
(b) Time spent on established products and new products. For example, 80 percent with current clients and 15 percent with prospects, 85 percent time on established products and 15 percent on new products.
(c) Objective should be established for target markets, ideal clients, referrals, new business growth and servicing, client categories.

Step 3: Compare your selected objectives to see if any oppose each other.

Step 4: Be realistic. You will probably be adding objectives to an already busy to-do list.

Step 5: Select goals to achieve objectives that enable you work from within your comfort zone, win early and often and are achievable.

How do you review and monitor progress?

The primary purpose of reviewing and monitoring your plans is to alert yourself when changes are needed in sufficient time and to take the necessary actions to fix or revise. Reviewing provides for adequate oversight in a timely fashion with the least expenditure of time and effort.

Guidelines:

Identify the small number of factors that will have the greatest impact including time, resources, quality, and quantity. When monitoring your plans, ask the following questions:

What is likely to change?

    Problems and opportunities
    Uncertainties
    Unexpected events
    Failure and stoppages
    Human errors

How will I know how we are progressing?

    What type of progress reports do I require?
    How frequently do I require status reports?
    What type of visual displays do I need?
    What corrective action is required?
    Self-correction
    Management action
    Operation action

Reviewing and monitoring your plans is designed to close the loop and keep you on track toward accomplishing what you set out to do.

Case Study

CEO of a services firm spent a considerable amount of money on developing a strategy for his business. The consultants produced an impressive document in a nice binder with tabs for each session. The problem was the CEO, and his leadership could not figure out how to implement the strategy. We helped him with converting the strategy into business unit tactics followed by individual plans for each professional that aligned with the overall strategy. The leadership team is now able to monitor progress on a monthly basis and the feedback is used to update the business strategy. The leadership team also feels in control of the business and has a good plan to develop professionals.

Summary

- A strategic sales plan is your roadmap, in fact you probably already have a sales plan. This could be formal or informal in your mind, on a to-do list or your budgets and targets. Planning can be divided into two parts strategic, focusing on the future direction of the business and its environment and tactical focusing on the short-term time frame of one year.
- You need both strategic and tactical plans. The former leads to the latter, however, the two cannot be done at the same time.
- A major cause of stagnant growth is due to a business inability to effectively implement their tactical plans.
- I have seen businesses that do an OK job developing a strategic side but are unable to formulate and execute the right tactics.

CHAPTER 10

Setting and Achieving Big Goals

Not failure, but low aim, is a crime.

—Ernest Holmes

Rain making is about execution focusing on the right task and activities that bring in new business and retain customers. Success is achieved from setting big goals that propel your business and career forward. Many professionals process the capabilities to become effective rain maker, only few, however, actually succeed.

Financial services author David Mullins Jr. has noted that of the 20 percent of advisors who survive the first two years, only 5 percent ever reach the top of their game. This is consistent with other professional service business that I have researched and worked with. There are two reasons for so few professionals reaching the top, fear and unwillingness to pay the price of facing rejection.

Rain making is selling that requires deep motivation, which comes with a high degree of rejection. Second, not knowing how to build a business, or worst, building a business that limits growth.

What are the characteristics of top producers?

They understand the mathematics of selling.
They have a selling system.
They market relentlessly.
They are motivated to succeed.
They make establishing relationships a number top priority.

What is the Mathematics of Selling?

One of the reasons why many professionals struggle to become effective rain makers is that they don't know how to build a business or they build a business that limits their growth. Becoming a successful rain maker starts with understanding the mathematics of selling.

There are six elements to this:

Element 1—Prospect pipeline
Element 2—Centers of influences
Element 3—Retention
Element 4—Referrals
Element 5—Minimum target size
Element 6—Account development

Element 1 Maintain at least 100 qualified relationships

You should develop and maintain 100 to 150 names in your prospect pipeline if you are a new professional (3 years or less) and 50 to 100 for experienced professionals (3+ years of experience). Experienced professionals should maintain a 50/50 ratio mix between existing and prospective clients. These should be your ideal category "A" customers and prospects that generate 80 percent of your business.

Use your sales system to contact each client three to four times per year. Assume each visit lasts one hour—that's ten hour per year per client and five hour per year for each prospect across 100 relationships equals 1500 hours.

The average professional works approximately 2300 hours per years; this leaves 800 hours per year for administration and other stuff. There are simply not enough hours in a day to try to service every customer. To retain and develop these 100 relationships, you will need to spend 80 percent of your time on four key activities—results, relationships, retention, and referrals—Roger Sitkin's refers to these as four money making activities.

Element 2 Maintain 10 non client referral sources

You should develop and maintain 10 centers of influence (COI) and meet them at least once a quarter with the goal of obtaining three referral and introductions each quarter. This will generate 30 leads per quarter (120 per year). Assume 50 percent agree to meet; this is 15 meetings. If 50 percent (7) are qualified and enter your selling process and 50 percent (3) become clients each quarter (12 per year), depending on your average sales—this may be the only marketing you will need to do.

Element 3 Have 100 percent of your top 20 percent customers

The goal is to retain 100 percent of your top 20 percent of customers that produce 80 percent of your revenue. Retention includes client numbers and the associated revenue. With 100 percent retention, 80 percent of your revenue budget is already achieved, and your top 20 percent are your category "A" and "B" customers producing the bulk of your revenues.

Element 4 Generate 80 percent of new business from referral and introduction

Top performers engage in referral only selling, whilst 100 percent referrals are difficult to achieve and maintain, however, 80 percent business from referral and introductions from existing customers and centers of influence is a realistic target. First, you need to follow selling system to retain 100 percent of your desired clients. We will cover this later in this chapter. You also need element number two—10 non-client referral sources. Implementing these two things will help you build and maintain 100 to 150 qualified relationships in your sales pipeline.

Element 5 Continually raise your minimum account size

As your business and capabilities grow, so should your minimum account size. One of the ways I achieved this during my career was by targeting more complex accounts. When the great Ben Feldman started selling his goal was to close three cases a week, as his cases got bigger, so did his volume. As your business grows annually, remove the bottom 10 to 15 percent of clients and replace relationships and targets in your sales pipeline.

Element 6 100 percent full-time customers

You should work toward having 100 percent wallet share with of top 20 percent customers who make up 80 to 90 percent of your business. There are three ways to grow your business. First, you can increase the number of customers through new business development; second, you can increase the average size of your new business customers; third, increase the frequency customers purchase from you. Start by conducting regular reviews to educate and upgrade your existing customers.

By applying these six numeric elements, a professional can continually grow their business by adjusting each of these elements for their situation. If you wish to increase the size of your new client's accounts, focus on element 5 and raise your minimum target size. Require more sales, increase the number of referrals from existing customer (element 4) and introductions from centers of influence (element 2).

What type Selling System do you Need?

You can't achieve big goals without customer. In Chapter 4, we discussed creating a sales model and unique selling system.

We will now focus on designing and implementing this sales system to produce results. I refer to this as the GARD system—generate, acquisition, retention, and development. Figure 10.1 outlines the GARD process to transfer your six numeric elements into an action plan.

Generating Prospects, Leads and Introductions

There are only two ways to market and sell, the hard way and the easy way. The hard way is through cold calling, and the easy way is leveraging your existing customers for referrals and centers of influence and past clients. Ultimately 80 percent of your new business leads should be generated from centers of influence, referral, and introductions.

Generate

Develop

Acquire

Retain

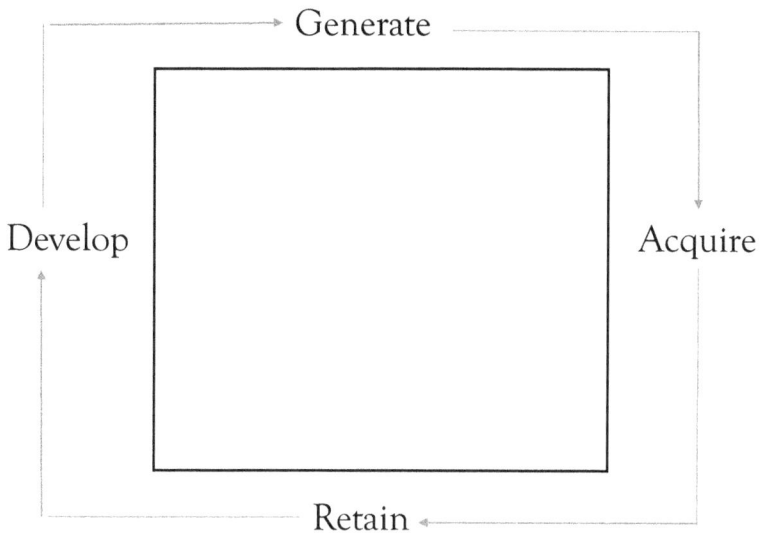

Figure 10.1 GARD framework

There is no marketing activity that is more effective than a proactive referral process. In fact, if you had to engage in only one form of marketing, a proactive referral process should be it. If you are in regular and frequent contact with your customers, have disciplined process and provide great service, you have the prerequisites for effective referral marketing. Appendix A provides a detailed referral marketing action plan.

For newer professionals with few customers, your initial lead generation should start by reaching out to people you already know—your known contacts.

Over time, as you build your customer base, get in the habit early of asking for referrals. Your primary lead generation process will consist of letters, phone calls, and networking.

Centers of influence

People from all walks of life can usually be developed into effective centers of influence—bankers, doctors, dentist, lawyers, schoolteachers, real estate agents, builders, agents, and tradespeople.

To develop centers of influence, make a list of everyone that you know, all of your contacts and LinkedIn connections. Select those who you feel would be a natural center of influence. This person does not need to be an intimate friend of yours to qualify as a COI, but they should have the following basic qualifications:

- They know you personally and a person who is willing to help you.
- They should have contact with the types of individuals you want to serve.
- They should have confidence in you and your ability
- They should have influence with the people recommended—a person whose judgement is sought after. Also, don't forget to add to your list the names of those people who did not qualify as a prospect. They may qualify as excellent COI. Appendix B provides a detailed action plan for obtaining centers of influence.

Acquiring: Converting prospects into meetings

The next part of the GARD model is converting leads into a meeting, and eventually, new business. A key skill for marketing success and building a successful business is the ability to obtain meetings with qualified prospects in person or virtually. Any activity that postpones this stage delays building the relationship; professionals who fear prospecting will do anything to get a feel-good response from a prospect and will delay rejection for as long as they can.

The essentials for acquiring new business:

> What is a qualified prospect? They have a need and you can make them see that their need is important enough to have you solve it. They have sufficient resources to do what is required to solve the need. They can be induced to invest the resources they can be persuaded to see that it makes sense to part with some resources. They represent those with whom you can work to the solution a reality.

Packaging Ideal customer profile:

Create a clear ideal client profile, target market (niche), location, size, and number of employees.

Package your expertise:

Top rain makers develop their expertise before approaching a prospective client. You can develop your expertise by researching your target market, speaking with prospective clients, contacting key influencers working in your niche market, and researching the issues, challenges, and concerns of prospective customer.

1. You job title: I'm an executive account director.

2. Your methodology : We have access to a dozen underwriters.

3. Your solution: The outcomes you deliver for clients.

4. Focus on their problems: The ideal outcome that people achieve by working with you or using your products and services.

Figure 10.2 Outlines the four ways to talk about yourself

Package your expertise in writing with articles and reports on your insights, speaking to targeted groups. Key items to include in your written packaging:

Executive summary

Personal bio

Product and service description

The time invested in developing your expertise will pay huge dividends as you approach your market as an expert and are able to distinguish yourself from others.

Verbal packaging

Prospects who don't know you personally have at least three questions they need answered before they consider meeting with you:

Who are you?

What do you do and for whom?

What value can you bring to my business?

Verbal packaging also known as value proposition helps you to describe what you do when someone ask what you do. Figure 10.2 outlines the four ways to talk about what you do.

Top professionals focus on a prospective customer problems and concerns. This is the most effective way that top rain makers package their expertise to reach out.

Proactive Reach Out

When first contacting a prospective customers, the first objective is to get a response, and second, getting a meeting to have a brief conversation. A mistake many professionals make is not knowing what they want to happen. Of course, everyone wants to receive a positive response from a prospect but are often unclear what that looks or sounds like. Among the various goals you can select are:

To contact a certain number of prospects each week.

To have one in 20 recipients call (that would be fabulous).

To have people recall receiving something from you.

To eventually land x percent meetings.

By following the lead generation process, you can select the prospecting activities that will work best for your particular situation.

Follow-up

Too many professionals give up too soon or worst don't follow up at all. For example, you might contact someone and get their voicemail, which is very likely these days. It can take on average five phone calls to actually reach your contact. In some cases, you may need to send a follow up e-mail if you haven't had a response base. You need to have follow-up mechanisms in place including voicemail script or follow-up e-mail or letter to send to a prospective customer.

Your lead generation process can happen quickly, or it can take a number of weeks, however, the ultimate goal is to make contact and have a conversation and moved them to your sales pipeline and to the acquisition process.

If you build your list as I described, you should expect to obtain between a 5 to 25 percent response rate from your list. Now, response rate doesn't necessarily mean that they are going to do business with you, but you avoid fence sitting and receive a yes, no or some sort of indication from them. As you get more experience and as the quality of your list improves and as you gain more referrals, about 50 percent you will have, you will get the 50 percent area, which is where a lot of top sellers operate from on referrals and centers of influence through the lead generation process.

Acquisition Stage

This is where you convert qualified leads into sales meetings appointments (phone, video, or face-to-face) and ultimately customer. Many professionals including myself conduct a good portion of their selling activities virtually. There are five acquisition steps:

Obtaining a meeting
Qualifying
Explore needs
Presenting solutions
Closing

Obtaining a Meeting (the Sales Discussion)

You want to obtain a meeting. This is simply asking that's been set for you and their previous process. During the meeting stage, you want to further qualify or verify if there is a fit, which leads us to step two. Firstly, does the client qualify not only for your products and services, but are you good fit for the individual you are working with and your business. The prospective client is also interviewing you.

Exploring Needs

During this stage, ask questions in detail to explore the needs. In the appendix, you will find questions to ask during this stage to drill down needs and qualify and determine where and how you can add value.

Presenting Solution

This is can be a two-step or more process depending on the complexity of your product or service. You may need to customize package your solutions, this is often a key differentiator with top professionals. On rare occasions, I have been in situations where I have gone through all the steps in one meeting, but for more complex sales and quality selling, it should be divided into two steps.

Besides if you have followed your process and have thoroughly qualified the client, they are not going anywhere. Where you are presenting your ideas, packaged your expertise, and presenting the customer solutions to make their situation much better than before they met you. This is where you outline how are you going to do and what you do.

Closing, Questions, and Objections

The close is nothing than a summation of the discussion. It should be nothing more than just a natural flow of the ideas you have been discussing, depending on your industry, in your marketplace, your products, and services. It's natural and welcoming when a prospective client has questions—that means they are interested. There is no excuse for not being prepared and anticipate prospective client's questions. The close should really be nothing more than a summation of what you have agreed upon. In the appendix, you will find the ten most common type of objections.

Retention

The third stage of the GARD framework is retention. 100 percent retention of your desired clients should be a primary goal if you are focusing on your ideal client profile category A and B with the potential to deliver 80 percent of your revenues over a period of time. These are the ones you want to maintain and retain over the long stage. These are the ones that are going to dramatically increase the value of your business, and you want to maximize the lifetime value of these clients. Retention process includes:

Planning
Deliver
Implementation
Review
Present
Continuation

Planning Stage

When a prospect is converted into a customer, they are transferred to your retention process. First, update your contact management system and client records. Depending on your service, set up a service calendar that aligns your continuation process to ensure the client is being contacted and updated.

Delivery

The actual physical delivery of your product or service. This delivery can be done in person or virtually. It's confirming that the service has commenced. I once purchased a new car, as I was swapping my old vehicle, someone from the dealership delivered my new car and drove my old one away. The next day, I received a call from the salesman from dealership who went through a checklist with me to confirm delivery. A similar approach can be developed for any type of product and service.

Review Stage

Some services may have a renewal date such as an insurance policy, annual contract, or subscription. Often unless there is a problem, there is no reason for the provider to contact you until the renewal. I recently contacted my phone carrier to discuss my plan and was surprised to learn my current plan was no longer offered and the newer plans offered more benefits and better coverage, but no one had bothered to contact me, I did change to a better plan to meet my needs that was cheaper and I also added on a couple of additional services. How much money are you leaving on the table by not conducting regular reviews with your customers to share new ideas, innovation, or simply update any changes in their circumstances? Depending on your product and service, this could be a midterm review where you learn a little bit more about your client professionally and personally.

Presenting Stage

When you discover gaps in a client's program this is an opportunity to present fresh ideas, not to sell but update providing an additional touch point, an opportunity to maintain your client relationships.

Continuation Stage

This is the education stage. Some professionals use events such as hosting a lunch or dinner for their best customers to educate them about trends, issues that can be actually fun nights. Some professionals do wine tasting, book signings, it's a great way to get your customers together to network with each other. It's also a nice way to ask for referrals indirectly by inviting your clients to bring along their friends and colleagues. The continuation stage is to continue the relationship and not simply renew.

Use the GARD Model framework to execute your plans and strategies.

Case Study

JB runs a mid-size insurance and financial services business specializing in family owned business. The firm's revenue had flat lined for the past three years and organic growth was negative. Whilst new business growth was slow, the big issue was the retention rate, which had slipped from the mid 90's to the high 80's. The firm had several long-term clients, however, unless there was an issue, the client would only be seen at renewal time. The GARD model was introduced, and all the key accounts were visited several times during the year. Within 12 months, referrals from key accounts increased driving up new business production and retention rates improves into the low 90's while cross selling additional services to existing clients improved.

Summary

Rain making is selling that requires deep motivation, which comes with a high degree of rejection. Second, not knowing how to build a business, or worst building a business that limits growth.

One of the reasons why many professionals struggle to become effective rain makers is that they don't know how to build a business or they build a business that limits their growth.

Becoming a successful rain maker starts with understanding the mathematics of selling. There are six elements.

Element 1—Prospect pipeline
Element 2—Centers of influence
Element 3—Retention
Element 4—Referrals
Element 5—Minimum target size
Element 6—Account development

CHAPTER 11

What Is Accountability?

We would accomplish many more things if we did not think of them as impossible.

—C. Malesherbes

When I arrive at the gym for my morning workout, there are usually several personal trainers helping their clients with the exercise routines. The main job of a personal trainer is holding clients accountable to achieve their fitness goals.

The highest performing businesses are those that set high performance standards and then hold their professionals accountable to those high standards. It begins with sales leaders and executives walking the talk and being openly accountable to the standards they set for themselves, and typically everyone else follows suit.

Building an accountability is often easier said than done. For rain makers, a culture of accountability includes, establishing objectives, preparing sales plans, motivation, and rewards.

What Are Objectives?

Great sales leadership begins with everyone setting specific goals. Goal setting is one of the activities most highly correlated to the success of top performers. Best Practices Insurance study found financial services businesses that are effective at goal setting grow roughly twice as fast as those that are not. Goal setting involves more than just establishing new business numbers, it is also helping professionals determine their focus (niche markets). An effective goal-setting process should get professionals focused in the areas holding the best potential for them.

What Are Sales Action Plans?

Coordination of sales plans assures that everyone is not *stepping on each other* and that opportunities are not being missed. Goals are the foundation for developing strategic sales action plans—which is the end product. The best sales plans include both activity goals and result goals. It is difficult to hold someone accountable or even to know how best to support and equip them without effective goal setting.

Sales action plans are usually determined by using one or a combination of the following approaches:

A series of activities
Problem solving approach
A series of smaller short-term objectives

A Series of Activities or Events

These are not necessarily inter-related, however, they will relate to the accomplishment of your overall objective. For example, becoming the market leader within your niche could include any of the following activities or events:

Becoming a member of the trade association
Developing a special report to send out to members
Speaking at conferences
Sponsoring events
Researching problems, issues, and concerns of key players

A Problem-Solving Approach

You have first clearly identified a problem that needs to be overcome. You have been analyzed to determine the appropriate course of action, which, if implemented successfully and sequentially, will lead to the eventual accomplishment of your objective, for example, an increase in your retention rate might include:

Compiling a list of all lost customers.

Identify reasons why they left, service, product, or relationship.
Identify vulnerable existing client relationships.
Create action plan to correct any issues with existing customers.
Retraining employees to improve future performance.

A Series of Smaller Short-Term Objectives

These breakdown the objective into smaller pieces of the larger result.
A good example of this type would be new business annual sales goals:

Breaking sales plan into quarterly objectives
Show by branch and individual
Break figures into monthly results
Weekly activity plans
Daily activity

What goes into a sales action plan?

Once you decided on a course of action, you intend to follow in the long-
term perspective of sequence of activities or events and an order in which
to work, so that you can begin to concentrate your efforts on what needs
to be accomplished in the short run. This does not need to be an elabo-
rate detailed action plan, however, it should be easy to identify significant
milestones and to make significant modifications as your proceed.

Action Plan Format

Long Term Objective: To have a minimum of $500k in client revenue within three years.
(Current year's revenue = $175,000 as baseline)

	What	When	How Much	Who	On Track?
1.	Generate minimum income from existing clients (Short term action plan needed)				
	a. $50,000				
	b. $75,000	Year 1	10 hrs/mo	JW	Monthly results
	c. $100,000	Year 2	10 hrs/mo		
2.	Generate minimum new business income from referrals. (Short action plan needed)	Year 3	10 hrs/mo		
	a. 25%	Year 1	10 hrs/mo		
	b. 50%	Year 2	10 hrs/mo	" "	" "
	c. 75%	Year 3	10 hrs/mo		
3.	Generate minimum new business leads from center of influence network.				
	a. 25%	Year 1	10 hrs/mo		
	b. 40%	Year 2	10 hrs/mo	" "	" "
	c. 80%	Year 3	10 hrs/mo		

Figure 11.1 Strategic action plan

What About Compensation Plans?

To attract and retain top professionals, a business needs to develop an attractive compensation package. Top professionals like income regularity, extra reward for above average performance, and fair payment for experience and longevity. Your business also would like to achieve growth, economy, and simplicity. Sometimes business objectives such as growth may conflict with a professional's objective such as financial security and this is a major reason why compensation plans can vary tremendously from industry to industry and even within the same industry.

Three compensation approaches:

Straight salary

Straight commission

Salary and commission

Straight Salary

Straight salary plans have several advantages they provide professionals with a secure income and this makes it more willing for to perform the nonselling activities and give less incentive to overlook key customers. From a business perspective, they provide simplicity and help lower turnover.

Straight Commission

The advantages of straight commission (commission only) plans is that they attract higher sales performance, provide more motivation, require less supervision, and control selling costs.

Combination Plans

Combination plans feature the benefits of both straight salary and commission plans while reducing their disadvantages. They are designed to provide the safety and security that someone needs, by providing a secure income it also provides the incentive to exceed objectives and the incentives can linked to a wide variety of goals and priorities.

Compensation Mix

After deciding your approach, the next step is to determine the mix. There are four options:

1. Fixed amount
2. Variable amount
3. Expense allowance
4. Benefits

Fixed amount salary—Intended to satisfy the professional's need for income stability.

Variable amount—Which might comprise of commission, bonus, or profit sharing, and is intended to stimulate and reward for greater effort.

Expense allowance—Enable the professional to meet expenses involved in travel and lodging and entertainment.

Benefits—Include paid vacations, sickness or accident benefits, pensions and life insurance. These are intended to provide security and job satisfaction.

Motivation

The most critical ingredient in sales leadership is investing the time required to identify promising salespeople. Bill Belichick is considered as one of the greatest coaches in NFL history with six Super Bowl titles coaching the New England Patriots for the almost 20 years. He spends as much time recruiting as coaching, scouring the landscape for the unique blend of talent, character, perseverance, teamwork, and strength to continue to build his team.

Great sales leaders continually prepare, they understand their overall business strategy and what is required of professionals for the business to achieve its growth objectives. Similarly, to a winning sports coach, great sales leaders begin preparing their team in training. They know what needs to be covered to develop their professionals to a required level.

They also take pride. Personally, I have been a sales leader, educator, and coach inside and outside formal settings on sports teams and in the office. There is nothing like knowing you had a hand in the development of someone's career.

7 Step Accountability Formula

Top Performers' senior manager and owners recognize they must not only support the creation of a sales culture, but they must also personally engage in and contribute to the sales culture. Here are seven steps to build a culture of accountability:

1. Take Ownership

A common key to the success of top performing businesses is that someone has assumed ownership over sales leadership (on occasion more than one person), who is fully empowered with the authority to take responsibility for addressing the key components of sales leadership.

2. Measure What's to Be Managed

Unless a business has the ability to measure key business development activities and results, it is very difficult to manage them. Top Performers measure results with a level of detail that allows them to understand what is happening. In addition to tracking new business, they also track what accounts they have failed to write and why they failed. Further, while renewal results are important. Top Performers also want to know how changes in attrition (losing accounts) are impacting results. This is key because problems with renewal results are difficult to address without understanding the source of the problem.

3. Manage What You Measure

The Top Performers hold their people accountable for results. If results are not being achieved, top firms ratchet up accountability, monitoring, and focusing on the activity that drives results. This is achieved in a number of different ways. For example, regular sales meeting on a weekly or monthly basis, provide written feedback on the performance of each and all of the producers, which can have the added benefit of simultaneously providing perspective on how each producer compares with their peers.

4. Provide Help

When someone is falling short, the first step is to find out why and provide them the help needed. This could mean more training or education. For others, it may need to be a change in their sales focus or strategy. Still others may need additional support or to be partnered with another salesperson or technical resource that will help complement their weaknesses (and strengths). The best find ways to help their people succeed, which may involve removing organizational obstacles someone is facing or personal habits or actions that are limiting their success.

5. Have Courage

This is the Achilles heel for businesses that are not achieving superior results. Many leaders are too tolerant of poor performance, particularly when it is coming from a senior producer or executive. Top Performers recognize that until they are willing to address nonperformance, their words and threats are hollow and ineffective. The willingness to act also involves properly recognizing the superior performance of the agency's top producers. Treating your best and worst the same is a formula for mediocrity.

6. Raise Expectations

Many of the Average Performers have average results because their people are allowed to set average goals and management has average expectations. Top Performers, on the other hand, have gotten there by *raising the bar* on performance. One of the best ways to make such a transition is to introduce into a sleepy group of producers a *race-horse* or high performing producer who will redefine potential and excellence and light a fire under the rest of the producers. Complacency, comfort, and acceptance of poor results are a common problem within many average performers.

Great sales leadership frequently involves raising the bar on the definition of acceptable behavior and results. Provide direction. A top Performer Perspective "We changed our culture, which required us to remove those sales and service staff that were not willing to make that change with us. The key to our success is a stronger focus on sales throughout the organization and increased accountability of producers for new business development."

7. Get Buy-In From Everyone

Your business cannot develop a true sales culture unless there is buy-in to the need to be a real sales organization and to create a true sales culture. Those providing the actual sales leadership must be committed to it, but the ownership group must be totally committed as well. Trying to create superior sales results in an organization with a nonperforming ownership group or senior producer group is extremely difficult, if not impossible.

Case Study

A wealth advisory business had been experiencing stagnant low growth for three consecutive years. The leadership team had invested thousands of dollars into training with very little to show in terms of organic growth. The problem, whilst management invested money into training—the advisors were left to own their own devices to implement their learning to grow their portfolio. The leaders started managing what they measured through weekly meetings with their advisors to better track activity. The regular feedback started holding people accountable eliminating excuses and procrastination, within 60 days, activity levels improved and within 12 months, the business posted positive growth for the first time in three years.

Summary

The highest performing businesses are those that set high performance standards and then hold their producers accountable to those high standards.

It starts with sales leadership, when the leadership team walks the talk and is openly accountable to the standards they set for themselves, and typically everyone else follows suit. Building an accountability is often easier said than done. For rain makers, a culture of accountability includes, establishing objectives, preparing sales plans, motivation, and rewards.

Accountability involves:

- Taking ownership
- Measuring what's to be managed
- Managing What You Measure
- Providing Help
- Courage
- Raising Expectations
- Obtaining buy-in

CHAPTER 12

Preparing for Sales Leadership: Focus to Drive Growth

Seeking mastery is a process and not an event.

—Gary Keller

A top priority for sales leaders is developing their professionals from simply doing work and passive business development into effective rain makers who are able to consistently acquire, retain, and develop customers to grow the business by better sensing, selling, serving, and satisfying the needs of their desirable customers.

Successful selling is not something that is done haphazardly. Instead, it should an integral part of your business in everything that you do. When this is achieved, your existing customers become part of your own private proprietary marketing system that will provide you with a distinctive competitive advantage.

Rain making is about building a marketing system that you will never outgrow, incorporating the strategies and guidelines discussed in the previous chapters to form the core of your unique development process. Over the past 20 plus years of developing my own rain making capabilities, leading professional teams and helping scores of professionals, I have discovered five principals sales leaders need to implement to open a world of possibilities for their business:

Action plans that make process the focus
Make progress the focus
Use accountability to sustain focus
Blocking time to maintain focus
Creating the right environment to sustain focus

How Do You Create Plans That Make Process The Focus?

Big goals keep your feet moving and lead you closer to realizing your business's full potential, however, big goals require big models and processes to achieve them. Action plans are a means to an end, not the end. All too often professionals to start out with great fanfare achieved great growth results and then hit a ceiling. Early in career, my boss held a sales meeting every Friday afternoon, he would publish everyone's weekly and monthly result, and no one wanted their name to be on the bottom of the list. That deadline would spur me into action, and I would always find a way to make a sale by Thursday afternoon or Friday morning at the latest. My boss nicknamed me My man Friday.

Effective sales action plans for professionals contain three elements:

Acquisition of new customers
Retention of existing customers
Developing customers into 100 percent full-time customers

Acquisition Plans

List the pro-active approaches you will use to build an overflowing sales pipeline filled with your ideal customers. I meet professionals who often brag they obtain all of their new business from referrals, which on the surface may be true, however, what I have found is that many of these same professionals are only receiving the occasional unsolicited referrals at best and even those are not to their ideal clients. It's one thing to obtain a referral and quite another to obtained quality referrals.

Professionals who fail to develop their acquisition capabilities wind up having to rely on ad hoc marketing approaches. Acquisition plans should include the following to generate a steady stream of leads and new clients:

- Generating referrals from existing customers
- Establishing a sufficient number of target of influences to provide leads
- Networking with professional industry associations to build your brand and establish key relationships.

Table 12.1 Client referral worksheet

Target Client Worksheet	Criteria
Where are they located?	
Industry	
Size	
Needs	
Experience with your type of services	
What problems, challenges and issues they are facing?	

Implement your acquisition plan by educating your existing top customers and referral sources on what an ideal customer looks like for you. Use the ideal client worksheet given in Table 12.1.

Retention Plans

The second part of your action plan is the retention of existing customers, without this, your your business development efforts will become a revolving door, customer coming in one door and out the other. The ultimate goal of a retention plan is to build a protection ring around your top 20 percent of clients that generate 80 percent of your revenues.

> I know of one firm that was struggling with a 50 percent retention rate with business going out the door faster than what they could bring it in.

Your goal, retain 100 percent of all of your desirable customers. Retention plans should include:

- Customers service plans—Goals for referrals, cross selling, and value adding ideas
- Pro-active contact—Update key decision makers throughout the year
- Customer service calendar—Schedule to get things done

A retention plan will guarantee your revenue providing a foundation for solid growth each year.

Development Plans

Converting your top 20 percent customers into full time customers by acquiring 100 percent share of their wallet. To achieve this, there needs to be a formal system (your continuation plan) to not only retain the customer but also expand your value offering.

How Do Use Accountability To Maintain Focus?

Everyone has skills and habits that at some point can create a natural ceiling, for example, a professional who regularly acquires new customers worth an average $1,000 but, has difficulty raising his average to $2,500 per account. Breaking through these barriers requires the ability to maintain this focus over time. Getting focus is actually easy, however, keeping it over time is not. The core models and systems to become a top professional are clearly identified in this book. Achieving top performance requires daily focus for as long it takes.

The reason long-term focus is difficult to maintain our minds begin to wonder, intellectual curiosity takes over, and before you know it, other things come up and prolonged focus on the same issue can feel like a routine and routine can lead to boredom, and when boredom sets in, attention drifts. When boredom sets in, the craving for something new starts to appear and more appealing, and before you know it, you are well off course and behind on your targets and budget. The lack of focus is a major reason why many professionals struggle with becoming rain makers. Smart professionals with the best intentions become easily distracted and involved in busy work that at times seems more interesting.

Busy work causes procrastination and the excuse "I'm too busy to sell." Focus brings results and long-term focus brings long-term results. Everyone has the ability to focus on something for a period of time.

The trick is to learn how to focus on something day in and day out for the long haul. The secret to achieving long-term results is focusing your efforts on the smallest number of key activities that will generate the greatest results.

A major league baseball team plays 162 games a year, and 81 of these are played on the road. Winning 100 games (0.600 winning percentage) in a season is considered a pretty good result and guarantees making the playoffs. One path for achieving 100 wins, winning 75 percent of home, and 50 percent of road games. This requires a daily focus on a small number of key activities such as keeping the players healthy and rotating pitchers. Similarly, a top professional focusing on the smallest key result areas, right priorities, and accountability to maintain focus on the right things.

Accountability is the most powerful tool for achieving big goals and long-term success. The role of a leader is to provide accountability by keeping track and then feeding it back. Accountability, picks up where time blocking leaves off. Your goal is to implement your plan, which is the focus. To achieve this you need to block out the time to do the key activities by ensuring business development is on your calendar; this provides the short-term focus. However, this still may not be enough, because long-term focus has to be maintained. The best way to have accountability is through a relationship that follows a process. Accountability shapes and reshapes your focus, providing a learning loop for seeing clearly what you should be focusing on and the feedback loop for refocusing when your attention slides. Figure 12.1 is an example of an accountability learning loop.

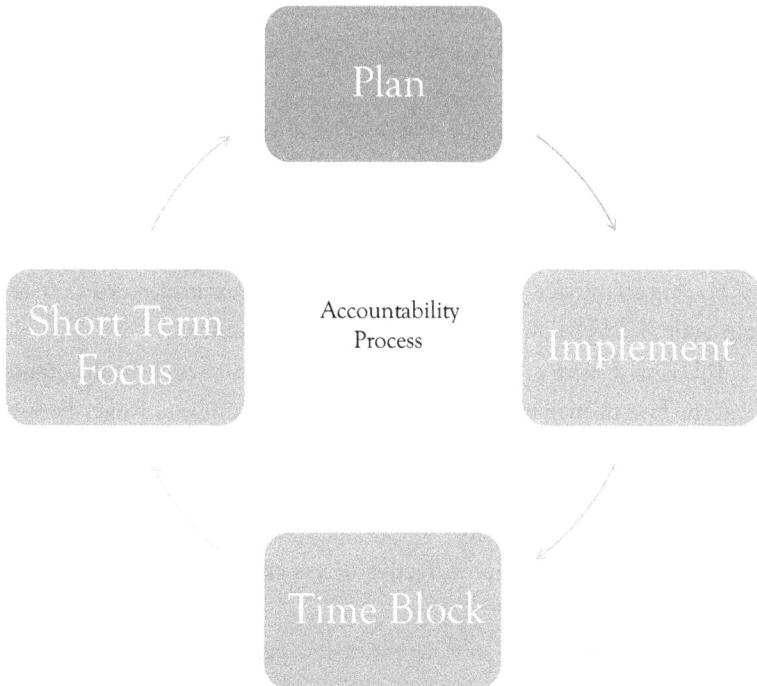

Figure 12.1 Accountability learning loop

This is tough to do on your own, so therefore, you need someone to hold you accountable, As the leader, your job is to hold your people accountable, but they must also know their numbers and keep track of those numbers, through monthly and weekly goals. Holding weekly meetings to assess and monitor progress is a step in the right direction.

Everyone Needs Feedback

For new professionals, coaching meeting should start off weekly and as they gain experience, this can be changed to biweekly or monthly, everyone needs feedback, professionals need to know the numbers and those who do not keep track of their acquisition, retention, and results performance will be hard pressed ever to sustain high levels of motivation and performance.

Your numbers and performance are about getting results and feedback. When a professional knows the results and the numbers, they can present those to you for discussion. The essence of the accountability feedback loop is to set your goals, do key activities, measure results, evaluate progress, and make adjustments and refocus as required, as shown in visual Figure 12.2. The more often you go through this process, the better your ability to fit.

To maintain focus on the activities that yield the best results, and to be effective, you must involve someone to hold you accountable and provide an outside perspective that strips away any excuses so you can see your actions, the results in a very honest manner.

Having an outside perspective strips away the excuses, so you can see your actions and results in a honest and clear manner.

This is why nearly all top professionals have coaches and consultants. Even the best of the best, Naomi Osaka, Lewis Hamilton, Roger Federer all have coaches to help keep them focused and on track to achieve their big goals.

Accountability is not just about maintaining focus: it is can also empower you to build more effective habits and awarness of when you are and aren't on track.

A monthly review of your activities and performance should be the minimum for all professionals.

```
        ┌─────────────────────┐ ◄──────────────┐
        │     Set Goals       │                │
        └─────────────────────┘                │
                  │                            │
                  ▼                            │
        ┌─────────────────────┐                │
        │    Do  Activities   │                │
        └─────────────────────┘                │
                  │                            │
                  ▼                            │  Refocus
        ┌─────────────────────┐                │
        │   Measure Results   │                │
        └─────────────────────┘                │
                  │                            │
                  ▼                            │
        ┌─────────────────────┐                │
        │      Evaluate       │                │
        └─────────────────────┘                │
                  │                            │
                  ▼                            │
        ┌─────────────────────┐                │
        │      Adjust         │────────────────┘
        └─────────────────────┘
```

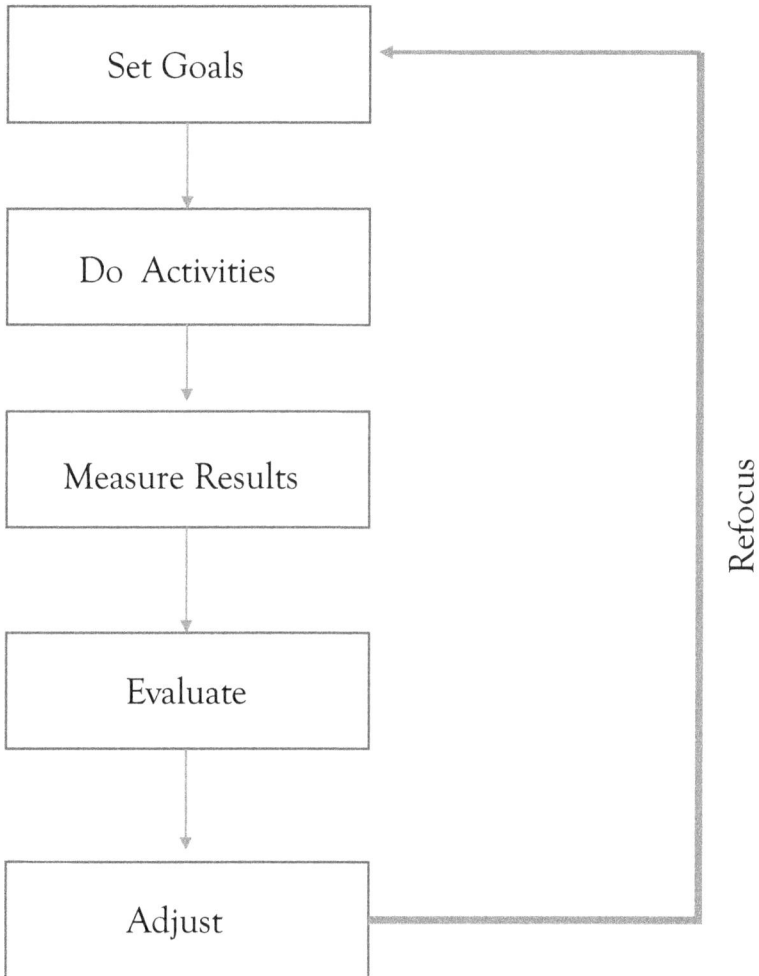

Figure 12.2 Accountability feedback loop

What Is Time Blocking?

Until your goals hit your calendar you won't consistently hit your goals. Time blocking helps you maintain focus and making sure you are able to get the key things done. Every professional has the same 24 hours in a day as everyone else, but it's so easy to fall into the busy trap when you are not clear on your model, not clear on your numbers or goals.

Time blocking is setting aside time in advance to accomplish the activities that will drive your results as a professional. For example, setting aside one hour per day to contact prospective clients and holding yourself accountable will help you maintain a steady flow of prospects to fill your sales pipeline. Time blocking is a process, a system to help you maintain your focus and leads to focus activity and high accomplishment.

Living Your Calendar

Top professionals don't have to-do lists, instead they have a have-to list and live in their calendar. This a very successful approach. It means instead of keeping that massive to-do list, a better approach is when you know something has come up and it's a priority item, immediately schedule that into your calendar. That's called living in your calendar.

Using this method, you will get more done because you are focusing on the most important activities that you need to do. Reserve time blocking for your top 20 percent activities that you must get done to produce your results. Practice and turn every key productivity habit into a time block, for every single thing that you do in your business. Professionals who never acquire this habit of time end up wasting time and focusing on the being busy instead of being productive. Top professionals are sensible enough to prioritize activities according to their ability to make their business grow and block time in their calendar to get things done.

How Do You Create The Right Environment?

Weather you realize it or not, your environment plays a huge part in your personal and business life. Your physical environment includes people, your space, your furniture, your equipment, your tools, supporting your efforts to keep you focused or do they distract you from achieving your task. I am surprised at how many people choose to tolerate a poor physical environment rather than to spend a little money to fix it. Invest in good equipment, purchase decent computers, phones, office chairs, and so on.

Monitor your business environment, you are your own gatekeeper and control what you let into your world. High achievers tend to associate with energizers and synergize with people who support their goals and work well with them. When you find the people in your life who are not in synergy with your goals, you will end up negotiating and compromising yourself.

Case Study

BZ runs a mid-size financial services firm with 15 professionals responsible for business development. As a leader, BZ was frustrated with the peaks and valleys in production across the business, she's a top-flight rain maker and thought everyone should be able to follow her lead, everyone in business admired and wanted to be like her. I explained the importance of making time for each of her professionals, setting aside just 15 to 20 minutes blocks for one-to-one time with each professional, three hours every other week reviewing plans, providing coaching, and mentoring.

The results were immediate, professionals appreciated and craved the feedback and she discovered areas where she could and should be providing help. Now BZ blocks out 30 percent of her time for coaching and mentoring, she has been able to reduce her client workload by assigning clients to other professionals with her guidance. Revenues, retention, and client referrals have increased.

Summary

- A top priority for sales leaders is developing their professionals from simply doing work and passive business development into effective rain makers.
- Rain making is about building a marketing system that you will never outgrow. Five principals sales leaders need to implement to open a world of possibilities for their business:
- Action plan make process the focus
- Make progress the focus
- Use accountability to sustain focusBlocking time to maintain focus
- Creating the right environment focus

Conclusion

Becoming a Rain maker

Selling is a key fundamental to every successful business. Professionals who do a great job of bringing in new business are more than just a salesperson. They are able to see a customer's big picture, they see opportunities for new services, to expand into new markets, create new offerings, and establish alliances, because they understand most of these ideas come from the market.

Salespeople are often the visionaries of their business as they are able to spot market changes to which the business must adjust. They have special abilities that make possible the way of life for their business and community they are a part of.

The objective of this book is to give you as a manager an understanding and tools to develop your professionals. Marketing is a numbers game that requires working through many small losses to win. It takes discipline to keep yourself in the market. If a person has discipline and motivation, then they too, can become a rain maker.

Selling is a noble profession!

Appendix A

Sales Capability Assessment

For each of the following statement put a ✓ in the appropriate column

	Disagree	Neither agree nor disagree	Agree
1. **Selling System**—You follow a formal sales process for new and existing business.			
2. **Prospect Pipeline**—You have identified what a future great client looks like and have an overflowing pipeline.			
3. **Time Focus**—You spend at least 80% of your available time on sales related activities.			
4. **Relationship management**—5 Key Areas: Clients, Prospects, Underwriters, Team Members, and Centers of Influence are formally identified and a program to manage in place.			
5. **Referrals/Introductions**—75% or more of new business comes from either a referral or introduction. You regularly practice asking for referrals and intros.			
6. **Account Development**—Goal is 100% of clients are *full-time* clients. You have a formal system of following up on part time clients.			
7. **Retention Strategies**—You follow a formal review process for the top 20% of accounts, to make sure that there are retention strategies in place.			

	Disagree	Neither agree nor disagree	Agree
8. **Centers of Influence**—You have 10 Centers of Influence with quarterly face to face visit or interaction.			
9. **Targeted Account Size**—You have a targeted account size for your individual pipeline.			
10. **Specialist vs. Generalist**—Identified various classes of business that you have become or in the process of being specialist.			
My Top Three Priorities	Ideas for Improvement		
1.			
2.			
3.			

Appendix B

Developing Center of Influences

One of the best ways to reach out by obtaining warm leads is through a system of centers of influences or co-operators, as they are sometimes referred to. These are nonclient referral sources. These are people who may never buy from you, but they are connected to individuals who will make great clients for you.

Begin by making a list of everyone you know, all of your contacts and LinkedIn connections.

Select those who feel would be a natural center of influence. This person does not need to be an intimate friend to qualify as a COI, but they should have the following basic qualifications:

- They know you personally and would be willing to help you.
- They should have contact with the types of individuals and markets you want to serve.
- They should have confidence and respect in you and your ability.
- They should have influence with the people recommended—a person whose judgement is respected.

People from all walks of life can usually be developed into effective centers of influences for you.

There are five ways to develop centers of influences:

1. Professional relationships
2. Personal relationships
3. Trade associations
4. Memberships
5. Research

Professional relationships

- Existing clients
- Past clients
- Past prospects

Personal relationships

- Social media
- Contact list
- Account, lawyer, and doctor

Trade associations

- Members
- Trade association executives
- Board members

Memberships

- Health club
- Networking groups
- Church, Rotary club, alumni

Research

- Journalist
- Analyst
- Publishers

Example: COI for a financial services professional could consist of real estate agent, a banker, accountant, lawyer; they would all have something in common, that is, servicing a similar type of client.

Appendix C

Developing Centers of Influences

Center of influences make selling easier by keeping your sales pipeline full with qualified names and introductions. It is said that the sales you close tomorrow depend on the kinds of doors that you open today. The following is a five- step approach to more doors to preferred prospects and warm leads:

1. Get names
2. Qualify
3. Obtain permission
4. Contact
5. Follow up

Start building centers of influences early in your career, strive for at least 10 that you meet with quarterly.

If you meet 10 centers of influences quarterly and each one gives you three names, that is 120 names a year. If 50% agreed to meet with you, that's 60 meetings; of those, 30 (50%) are qualified, 15 (50%) agree to do business with you. That is more than one new client per month with very little effort and resources on your part, you have simply built your network and asked the questions of your centers of influences and followed up. COI marketing is so powerful and why you want to, as your career progressed, that 80% of your business should be coming from these types of sources.

Appendix D

90 + Client and Prospect Questions

To improve your knowledge about your customers and prospects.

Client Profile

Name Company
Contact (Buyer)
Title
Category (A-B-C)
Revenue
Percentage of total revenues
Last contact
Next contact
E-mail
Phone: Direct—Mobile—Office
Website / LinkedIn/Twitter
Address Mailing Address
Industry
ANZSIC Code (s)
Description
Client since
Source (where did they come from)

Professional Background

1. Describe your position.
2. How long have you owned or been with your company?
3. Describe your background—what did you do before you started, bought, or came into this business?
4. Describe exactly who the owner or owners are.

5. What people, books, and life factors have influenced and impacted you in your career?

6. What are your goals?

7. What initially got you started in your business? (What motivation, occurrence, etc.?)

8. How have your methods for doing business, or the product(s) or service line(s) you market, changed since the inception of your business?

9. What do you do when you are not at the office?

10. Describe your family. Are you married? Are you divorced? How many children do you have?

11. What is the greatest life achievement you have achieved so far?

12. What one thing, more than anything else, do you want to accomplish in your business before you get out?

13. Where do you see your industry in five years?

14. What is your vision for your business for the next: 6 months, 1 year, 3 to 5 years, 10 years?

Business Profile

15. Describe what your business does completely. Products and services you sell and how you sell them? Who do you sell to by industry?

16. Specific niche?

17. Where does most of your business come from?

18. Product or service

19. Category of customer

20. Geography

21. Who has the highest propensity of buying from you?

22. What is your business philosophy as it relates to your customers?

23. When was the last time you introduced a new product or service to your market (both existing customers and prospects)?
    - How well did it work?

24. Describe your company's general infrastructure.
    - What Departments do you have? Operations/Marketing/Sales/Legal/HR and so on.

25. Who runs things? Who are the decision makers? (For example: "I own the business but I am never there, and I defer to my manager.")

Company Infrastructure Diagram

26. Please provide a visual diagram of your current organizational structure.
27. How do you explain your company to someone outside your industry?
28. Describe your company in one sentence.
29. How do you explain your company to someone in the industry (i.e., to a potential buyer or client)? This is the *company pitch*, NOT the product pitch.

Client Base

30. How many active customers do you have?
31. Exactly what kind of data do you have on them? (Include everything you know about your customers: names, addresses, telephone numbers, fax numbers, e-mail addresses, types of businesses, location, what and when they have bought from you, how you attracted them, the last date of contact with them, etc.)
32. How many *dream* clients are there (that 20% that would drive 80% of your sales)?
33. What does it cost you to set up a new customer? (E.g., if you ran an advertisement that costs $1,000 and you attained two new customers, it would be $500.)
34. What are the average sales and profits generated from a new customer in the first year? How is that information useful in your overall marketing strategy?
35. What is the *lifetime value* of your typical customer? (I.e., how much revenue will he/she generate for you over the entire period he/she does business with your company?)
36. Explain where all your business is coming from (demographics) versus where all your time is being spent.
37. What is your biggest and best source of new business?
38. As a percentage, how much of your business comes from referrals?

Sales Force

39. Selling infrastructure
40. Describe your sales team
41. Do you have inside sales—people?
42. Who does what?
43. What the best excels at and what the worst excels at?
44. What are their strengths and weaknesses, and where they are utilized?
45. What is your average order amount?
46. What are your sales (gross and net income) per salesperson? Is that above, below, or equal to your industry average and what are the steps you are taking (or going to take) to improve?
47. What are the standards for hiring salespeople?
48. What other training do you offer (i.e., product training, account management training, or time management training)?
49. How is it offered (internally, externally, etc.)?
50. How often is training provided?
51. What is the turnover rate for salespeople?
52. Describe the typical sales cycle to close a sale (i.e., from generating the lead through to a close):
    a. How many contacts does it take to close a sale?
    b. How many different people do you usually meet with to close a sale?
53. Describe the length of cycle from initial contact to close?
54. What are the most frequent objections you hear?
55. If you target 10 prospects, how many will you close? (Provide the closing ratio.)
56. As a percentage, with how many clients are you dealing with directly with the top decision maker?
57. What are the top three reasons that a prospect would do nothing at the end of the sales cycle?
58. What do you do with the prospects you don't close?
59. How do your closing ratios fare against that of competitors?
60. Do you utilize another form of direct sales (i.e., independent sales reps, dealers, manufacturer's reps)? If you do, have you ever compared the results to an inside or outside sales force?

61. Do you go to trade shows? What do you do, and how do you show? What is your preparatory approach? What promotions do you do in conjunction with trade shows?

62. What is your selling presentation?

63. How many unsold prospects do you have?

64. What sales functions did you perform when you started your business?

65. Do you add on other products or future products or services (up sell)?

66. How long does it take you to fill an order after you receive it? If you improved, would it have a dramatic effect on your sales?

67. Is *buyer's remorse* a current problem in your business? If so, how do you overcome it?

68. Do your customers feel your customer service department is prompt and courteous? Explain.

Marketing

69. What is your target market and how did you arrive at it?

70. What is your market potential (universe)? What is your current share of that market?

71. Does your business market locally, regionally, nationally, or internationally?

72. What change is required to satisfy the projected vision of your business?

73. Describe the company's marketing philosophy.

Strategic Partners

74. What strategic alliances do you currently have?

75. What strategic alliances did you have in the past?
    - How did they fare?
    - How did they affect your business?

76. Who stands to gain more than you if you grow? (I.e., companies whose products/services are purchased after your products/services are purchased. Companies whose products/services are concurrently purchased with your product/service.)

77. Who are your suppliers or other providers of products or services that benefit massively when you are successful?
78. Unique Selling Proposition (USP)
79. What do you believe is your single most competitive advantage?
80. What problem does your product or service solve for the customer?
81. Describe your customer's needs and the positive results your product/service provides.
82. What is your Unique Selling Proposition or USP?
83. Why do your customers buy from you?
84. What is it about your product and/or service that distinguishes you from your competition?
85. Why must a prospect buy your product or service?

Competition Profile

86. Describe all you know about your competitors.
87. Where are the top 3 located?
88. What do they do best?
89. What do they do worst?
90. How do you specifically fill that void?
91. What do they offer that you do not?
92. What steps do you take to offset their advantage?
93. What is the biggest customer complaint about your industry? How does your company address this problem?

Suggested Reading List

	Fast Company
	Forbes
	Inc Magazine
	Industry publication for their specific industry
	Selling Power
	Wall Street Journal
	Wired
Bellman, Geoffrey	The Consultants Calling

Conner, Dick	Getting New Clients
Duhigg, Charles	The Power of Habit
Geraghty, Barbara	Visionary Selling
Goldsmith, Marshall	What Got You Here Won't Get You There in Sales
Harding, Ford	Rain Making
Heinecke Stu	How to Get a Meeting with Anyone
Keller, Gary	The One Thing
Konrath, Jill	Selling to Big Companies
McLaughlin, Michael	Winning the Professional Service Sale
Mullen, David J.	The Million Dollar Financial Services Practices
Nadler, Gerald	Smart Questions
Pink, Dan	To Sell is Human
Rackman, Neil	Major Account Sales Strategy
Sinek, Simon	Start with Why
Sullivan, Dan	The Advisor Century
Tracy, Brian	Advanced Selling Strategies
Warren, Clifton	Financial Services Sales Handbook

About the Author

Clifton Warren is the principal of Clifton Warren Consulting; his firm trains professionals to market, sell, and win new clients. He is the author of Financial Services Sales Handbook and Cross Selling Financial Services. His articles and columns appear in industry journals and his monthly newsletter is read globally by professionals. Originally from California, he resides in Melbourne Australia. Contact Clifton at www.cliftonwarren.com

Index

OTHER TITLES IN THE SELLING AND SALES FORCE MANAGEMENT COLLECTION

Naresh Malhotra, Georgia Tech, Editor

- *How to be a Better Deal-Closer* by Simon P. Haigh
- *Entrepreneurial Selling* by Vincent Onyemah
- *Selling: The New Norm* by Drew Stevens
- *Creating Effective Sales and Marketing Relationships* by Kenneth Le Meunier-FitzHugh, Le Meunier-FitzHugh, and Leslie Caroline
- *Improving Sales and Marketing Collaboration* by Avinash Malshe and Wim Biemans
- *Competitive Intelligence and the Sales Force* by Joel Le Bon
- *Key Account Management* by Joel Le Bon and Carl Herman
- *Effective Sales Force Automation and Customer Relationship Management* by Raj Agnihotri and Adam Rapp
- *Sales Technology* by Nikolaos Panagopoulos
- *A Guide to Sales Management* by Massimo Parravicini
- *Lean Applications in Sales* by Jaideep Motwani and Rob Ptacek

Announcing the Business Expert Press Digital Library

Concise e-books business students need for classroom and research

This book can also be purchased in an e-book collection by your library as

- a one-time purchase,
- that is owned forever,
- allows for simultaneous readers,
- has no restrictions on printing, and
- can be downloaded as PDFs from within the library community.

Our digital library collections are a great solution to beat the rising cost of textbooks. E-books can be loaded into their course management systems or onto students' e-book readers.
The **Business Expert Press** digital libraries are very affordable, with no obligation to buy in future years. For more information, please visit **www.businessexpertpress.com/librarians**. To set up a trial in the United States, please email **sales@businessexpertpress.com**.

www.ingramcontent.com/pod-product-compliance
Lightning Source LLC
Chambersburg PA
CBHW061318220326
41599CB00026B/4932